SPEAK FREEDOM

Developing Emergent Leaders in the Struggle for Justice

K. Randel Everett

Dallas, Texas

Speak Freedom: *Developing Emergent Leaders in the Struggle for Justice*

BAPTISTWAY PRESS® Leadership Team
Executive Director, Texas Baptists: David Hardage
Associate Executive Director, Texas Baptists: Craig Christina
Director, Center for Church Health, Texas Baptists: Phil Miller
Publisher, BaptistWay Press®: Bob Billups
Marketing Coordinator, BaptistWay Press®: Stan Granberry
Publishing Specialist, BaptistWay Press®: Nancy Feaster

Cover Design: Meryl Randman
Production, Design, and Printing: Randall House

Ordering Information: www.baptistwaypress.org

First edition: February 2021

ISBN-13: 978-1-948618-42-7

Book Endorsements

As stated by Thomas Paine, "These are the times that try men's souls." *Speak Freedom* is a timely book that helps to make clear the types of leaders needed for the challenging times in which we live. The reader will be challenged to embrace their role and their place in the world. The author's enlightened examination of the topic of "Leadership" will challenge you to learn and enhance your own budding qualities as a leader in times of calm and crisis.

—Dr. Michael A. Evans, Sr.,
Senior Pastor of the Bethlehem Baptist Church,
and Mayor of Mansfield, TX

Speak Freedom is a timely classic during this challenging season. Dr. Everett is not only teaching about leadership quality as visionary, risk-taking, passionate, creative, and courageous. He lives through it. Anyone who seeks a biblical perspective with practical illuminations should read this book.

—Dr. Bob Fu, author of *God's Double Agent*,
Founder and President of China Aid

In today's world, more than ever, we need Christian role models in our communities for people of all ages, but particularly for our young people, who will be our leaders of tomorrow. Dr. Everett reminds us that transformational leaders must be passionate, competent, and strategic if they seek to bring about positive change to broken systems. I commend this book to those who aspire to offer hope for the world's most vulnerable and who, through a strong relationship with God, seek to effect change not only in our lives, but also turn our entire nation around.

—Drayton McLane, Jr.,
Chairman of the McLane Group

K. Randel Everett has spent a lifetime faithfully and fruitfully leading Christian congregations, institutions, and organizations. In *Speak Freedom*, he shares stirring stories about and foundational principles for leadership that will inspire and inform leaders young and old alike. Whether an emerging leader or one who is tried-and-true, this book will help you to become an increasingly effective leader. If you are looking to link your call to serve God sacrificially with leading others skillfully, *Speak Freedom* will prove to be both a gift and a goad.

—Todd D. Still, Ph.D.
Dean Truett Seminary, Baylor University

Jesus had two passions for the world beating in His heart. He had a passion for individuals, to love them and set them free. He also had a passion for challenging and changing social and institutional structures. That is why the establishment hated Him. A young leader said recently, "Silence is violence." That is what makes this book so special, its very title says, "Speak" and it says, "Speak Freedom." Randel Everett, like William Wilberforce before him, knows that equipping leaders with not only the tools, but also the passion, is essential for real change to occur. Religious freedom finds itself challenged around the world and people are suffering because of it. Whenever Jesus spoke with urgency and hope He always began with the word, "Today." Randel, thank you for raising up leaders who will speak freedom today.

—John Upton, Executive Director,
Baptist General Association of Virginia

In times like these, we need leaders to emerge to handle the many challenges we face in our world. *Speak Freedom* helps us understand the kinds of leaders who are essential for meeting these great tasks. The reader will be enriched and equipped by this book.

—Dr. Ralph West, Founder and Senior Pastor of
The Church Without Walls, Houston, Texas

As we face difficult times throughout the world, it is important that new leaders are being well trained, especially in the area of religious freedom. *Speak Freedom* makes clear the type of person that will be effective in leadership roles. They must be visionary, passionate, and courageous. I have great respect for Randel Everett who has the heart and knowledge for training such leaders.

—Former Congressman Frank Wolf from Virginia

Dedication

This book is dedicated to our adult children

Jeremy and Rachel,

both emergent leaders in the struggle for justice.

Contents

Foreword

Elijah M. Brown
General Secretary and CEO, Baptist World Alliance

In the midst of a raging storm, a lonely boat groaned under the weight of the wind and rain while those within responded with an understandable fear and uncertainty. When strategies and experience collapsed in the wall of crushing turbulence, it was the presence of Jesus and the willingness of these leaders to turn to Jesus—even with a faltering trust—that led to hope and renewal.

This story, recorded in Matthew 8, Mark 4, and Luke 8, is emblematic of leadership today. It often feels as if the structures and strategies that have guided our lives and organizations are floundering in the face of a furious storm, which has appeared as if without warning. Many are struggling with an overwhelming fear and doubt and a lack of clear direction.

That is why this book, *Speak Freedom: Developing Emergent Leaders in the Struggle for Justice,* is an essential tool for all leaders today, whether you are just launching in leadership or are a seasoned traveler. Born out of a lifetime of practical experience that has included growing churches in four different states, founding a seminary that has celebrated over twenty years of impact, serving as the CEO of one of the top ten largest Baptist denominations in the world, and most recently launching a nonprofit with a global reach that focuses on standing with the persecuted, in this timely writing Dr. Randel Everett provides the principles and the insights needed to navigate these unsettled times.

Not only is such leadership necessary in our own communities and organizations, *Speak Freedom* is a compelling call to pursue transformational leadership in partnership with many around the world who live in the most vulnerable contexts. To use just a few contemporary examples:

- 25 million people remain locked into modern-day slavery
- 75 million people struggle as refugees and displaced people
- Restrictions on religious freedom and persecution are on the rise globally
- Racism remains systematically embedded into many societies around the world
- Environmental degradation threatens whole communities
- 135 million continue to struggle with acute food insecurity.

Within the worldwide Baptist community, 13 million Baptists, or 27% of the 47 million Baptist World Alliance community live in situations of the greatest hunger, most pressing violent conflict, most restrictive religious freedom challenges, and the most difficult limitations on life expectancy, education availability, and average income. Baptists and all people of goodwill are called to honor the human dignity inherent in each person, and even when it seems impossible, to live as leaders pursuing peace and justice. For as Jesus says, "Blessed are the peacemakers, for they shall be called sons [and daughters] of God" (Matthew 5:9).

It is voices of vulnerability that we should allow to pierce through the stormy winds of resistance and guide us forward. As Deuteronomy 16:20 states, "Follow justice and justice alone" (NIV). For many, to embrace a model of leadership that prioritizes lasting transformation on behalf of those facing vulnerability, it will require a journey of change both within ourselves and within our organizations. *Speak Freedom* will give you the tools you need to lead with sacrificial impact. Drawing upon biblical insights and compelling multifaith leadership case studies from around the world, you will be guided along the three necessary paths required for meaningful change.

The first path is an inward reflection to strengthen your passion, clarify your vision, and focus on the elements of character that are foundational to this journey. The second path is developing a leadership of excellence that will enable you to communicate, organize, and build a team of high impact. The third path, the one most often neglected but most essential to genuine transformation, is how to institutionalize systemic change that leaves a lasting legacy and extends impact far beyond the reach of any one individual.

More than a theoretical framework, *Speak Freedom* is written as a practical resource to help you work through the challenges you face today in order to embrace a tomorrow that extends greater peace and justice for many. I have seen firsthand the impact of this teaching from community leaders in Ethiopia to church leaders under threat in China to national leaders in Washington, D.C.

Speak Freedom will equip you to navigate tumultuous storms, pursue sustained change in the winds of resistance, and live as a transformational leader with a legacy of standing together with the most vulnerable around the world in pursuit of freedom.

Introduction

They could hardly breathe. There was no air, it was dark, and the stench was suffocating. Where were they and where were they going? How long had it been since they were rounded up like animals, chained, and placed in the belly of the ship? The tossing of the waves coupled with the heat and empty stomachs brought vomiting and diarrhea and the pots provided for them to relieve themselves were too difficult to reach because they had to climb over the others who were crammed in beside them.

Fifty-four women and children were brought to the deck. The sun was blinding them and they were startled by the attention. The crew began to free them from their shackles. The freedom from chains that bound them and the fresh air they breathed after coming out of the belly of the ship brought a glimpse of hope. Was their nightmare about to end?

But then the unbelievable happened. The slaves were grabbed and thrown overboard into the sea. Two days later forty-two men were cast into the sea. By this time the slaves below were hearing the cries of those being thrown overboard and when thirty-six more men were gathered up and tossed into the water, ten others took their fate into their own hands and jumped to their deaths. Unscrupulous sailors drowned 132 Africans. One slave who was thrown overboard was able to catch a rope and pull himself back into the boat. He lived to tell the story of the fate of the others.

How is it possible that human lives were worth no more than cargo to be rounded up and sold as tools or drowned as useless freight? Even those who were fortunate enough to survive the journey were sentenced to a life serving at the pleasure of others who owned them as tools for the profit of their masters.

The Zong Incident was unfortunately not an isolated situation. The cargo ship, Zong, was just one of the many ships used for the trafficking of men, women, and children. The ship set sail from Accra, Ghana, on August 18, 1781, with 442 slaves on board, more than twice the number it could safely carry. The inexperienced captain of the ship was Dr. Luke Collingwood, a surgeon who had served on a previous ship in his role as a physician. The surgeon's responsibility was typically reserved for assessing the commodity value of a potential slave. If the slave was perceived to be of no value, the African traders who had captured him often killed and disposed of the useless slave.

Because of overcrowding and poor navigational skills the journey took longer than usual. Some slaves died while the ship was going along the African coast purchasing other slaves. Others died because of the inhuman conditions of the ship. The captain knowing that a dead slave was of no value, came up with the diabolical idea that if a slave died as a "Peril of the Sea," something beyond the captain's control, they were covered by insurance and the owner was reimbursed for his loss. Collingwood conjured the idea that the insurance company would be told there was a serious shortage of drinkable water because of the extended length of the journey and some slaves had to be sacrificed for the good of the others.

Some of the crew hesitated at the captain's command that slaves be thrown overboard. Even evil vile men caught up in the slave trade still had a tinge of a conscience yet for their own safety acquiesced to the diabolical plan and quickly gave in to the idea and participated in the murder of the slaves to protect their own lives. When the ship finally arrived at Black River, Jamaica, on December 22, 1781, only 208 slaves had survived the journey.

The ship's owner, James Gregson, filed a claim for their loss citing the ship did not have enough water to sustain the crew and the human commodities. The insurance company rejected the claim; yet in 1782, the Jamaican court ruled in favor of the owners.

The publicity of the Zong massacre reached the ears of Britain's abolitionists, especially Granville Sharp, who used the murder of the slaves to increase public awareness of the horrors of slavery. Sharp attempted to have criminal charges brought against the owner, captain, and crew of the Zong, but was unsuccessful. However the narrative about slavery was beginning to change. Other significant leaders, including the British Parliamentarian William Wilberforce was brought into the conversation. Wilberforce committed the rest of his life to the defeat of slavery. Just days before his death, Parliament abolished slavery throughout the British Empire in 1833.

The abolition of slavery was a victory for slaves in Britain, yet worldwide injustice must ever continue to be opposed in every generation and in every nation. Racism and oppression never rests. A Civil War was yet to be fought in the 1860's in the United States. In the 20th century in Europe, Nazis would kill over 6 million Jews and about 5 million non-Jews, including Roma, Jehovah's Witnesses, mentally handicapped, and others. A hundred years after slaves were freed in the U.S., Martin Luther King, Jr. and a host of other transformational leaders led a nonviolent revolution that exposed the inhumanity of segregation and the oppressive Jim Crow laws that punished Blacks for not being born white.

The philosopher George Santayana wrote, "Those who cannot remember the past are condemned to repeat it." On April 29, 2013, almost 1,000 survivors of the Nazi Holocaust as well as veterans of WWII joined former President Bill Clinton and Nobel Peace laureate Elie Wiesel to celebrate the 20th Anniversary of the U.S. Holocaust Memorial Museum. Those attending the anniversary received a black bag with the words, "**Never Again**," emblazoned on the front in large letters. Beneath them in smaller letters were the words, "What you do matters."[1]

Speak Freedom is about emergent leaders making a difference in cultures of resistance. Unfortunately, our world has not learned from our past. Hundreds of Baylor University students heard their favorite professor, Dr. Ralph Lynn, say, "We learn from history that we do not learn from history." Unjust systems continue unabated throughout many world cultures perpetuating cruelty while too often they are unchallenged by the silence of those unwilling to stand with the sufferers. Where are the *emergent leaders* driven by a passion for justice instilled in them by the love and righteous of God? Occasionally some appear on a global stage like William Wilberforce or Martin Luther King, Jr. However, others more often but with less notoriety, serve faithfully and at times in the shadows including nurses risking their own lives while caring for sick strangers; coaches teaching young athletes that integrity is more important than trophies; pastors preaching faithfully and practicing justice, humility and kindness; journalists speaking truth to power; elected officials fighting for the rights of the voiceless; and parents teaching their children to seek first the Kingdom of God and His righteousness.

During the past several years, the members of our team from 21Wilberforce have traveled to numerous countries of concern, interviewed hundreds of survivors of religious persecution, visited refugee camps and IDP (Internally Displaced People) camps across Africa and the Middle East, met with human rights leaders from every continent and learned that genocide, executions, coerced organ transplants, false imprisonment, kidnappings, and widespread discrimination continues in our world at an alarming pace. Even within so-called developed nations, including those in North America and Europe, systemic racism continues to oppress minorities. Authoritarian governments silence dissenters with brutality. Totalitarian governments, mobs, radical religious groups and even family members for no other reason than their beliefs kill thousands annually.

God's call to His people is always a call for justice. In Micah 6:8, the prophet declares, "He has told you, O man, what is good; And what does the Lord require of you but to do justice, to love kindness, and to walk humbly with your God?" In the Sermon on the Mount Jesus said, "But seek first His kingdom and His righteousness; and all these things will be added to you" (Matthew 6:33).

In 1999, Dee Hock, the founder of VISA, wrote the book, *Birth of the Chaordic Age*. On the inside cover of his book he defines *chaordic*, "The behavior of self-governing organism, organization or system which harmoniously blends characteristics of order and chaos."[2] If there was ever a time when we lived between chaos and order it is certainly the year 2020. The pandemic, natural disasters, wars, famine, mass migrations of people groups escaping violence, religious persecution, protests, and in many countries including the U.S., there has been a bitterly disputed election. Suffering communities are crying out globally asking the question, "Where are the leaders that will offer us hope?" *Speak Freedom* is a challenge for courageous men and women to stand up for justice in this era of crisis and lead.

The Oxford Dictionary defines *emergent*, "The process of coming into being or becoming prominent; or denoting a plant that is taller than the surrounding vegetation, especially a tall tree in a forest."[3] Our world desperately needs courageous *emergent leaders* who will stand above all others guiding us away from chaos and disorder to the hope that comes from righteousness; leaders who will resist evil and promote justice for all.

Speak Freedom is written from my perspective as a Christ follower believing that spiritual enlightenment must precede meaningful awakenings. A frightened group of ragtag followers of Jesus turned the world upside down within a generation of Christ's resurrection. By God's grace, Christ's followers of this generation have the same opportunity to participate in such a global impact. Are you willing for God to call you to join with Him in this spiritual awakening?

God's Spirit stirred the hearts of millions from the two continents of America and Europe during the Great Awakening. One of those whose eyes was opened was the British parliamentarian, William Wilberforce. He began to see slaves as individuals of worth, created in the image of God, rather than as soulless tools used for the profit of evil men. This led to his lifelong pursuit of the abolition of slavery.

Speak Freedom uses biblical, historical, contemporary, and personal examples of leaders who have brought about positive change within cultures of oppression that transcend their own time and place. The clearest example is Jesus who never forgot His mission, equipped the disciples to duplicate His ministry, and breathed life into the church that continues to take His message to the ends of the earth. Jesus refused to be sidetracked by public opinions, praise, criticism, and even execution. His influence didn't end with

His death but continues throughout the world two thousand years later because He equipped His followers to continue His work, in the power of the Spirit, to the ends of the world.

Biblical examples in addition to Jesus that are considered are Moses, Nehemiah, and the Apostle Paul. Individuals who have brought about systemic changes in recent history include William Wilberforce, Hannah More, and Martin Luther King, Jr. A host of contemporary leaders will also be discussed that are living courageous visionary lives seeking to bring systemic justice against generational oppression.

Effective leaders must be passionate, competent, and strategic. With that in mind, *Speak Freedom* has three primary components: Living with Passion, Leading with Excellence, and Leading Systemic Changes. All three are essential if transformation is to be sustained. *Speak Freedom* utilizes stories and best practices from proven leaders who are bringing light to a world of darkness.

Endnotes

1 The story of the Holocaust survivors was taken from an article in *The Georgetowner*, July 11, 2013, by Jeff Malet.

2 Dee Hock, *Birth of the Chaordic Age* (San Francisco, CA: Berrett-Koehler Publishers, 1999), inside cover.

3 Erin McKean, Editor in Chief, *Concise Oxford American Dictionary* (Oxford, England: Oxford University Press, 2006), 294.

Part 1

Living With Passion: How to Discern Your Kingdom Assignment

Jesus said...

"and you will know the truth, and the truth will make you free"

(John 8:32).

F'eedom!

Martin Luther King, Jr. spoke of the children that joined them for their demonstrations against segregation. The Civil Rights Movement was accused of using children as props. King responded, "The children themselves had the answer to the misguided sympathies of the press. One of the most ringing replies came from a child of no more than eight who walked with her mother one day in a demonstration. An amused policeman leaned down to her and said with mock gruffness: "What do you want?"

"The child looked into his eyes, unafraid, and gave her answer. '**F'eedom!**' she said."

"She could not even pronounce the word, but no Gabriel trumpet could have sounded a truer note."[1]

Men, women, and children from all over the world are crying out for freedom: Blacks in America crying out against systemic racism, religious prisoners being tortured for their beliefs, young girls living in the clutches of sex-traffickers, citizens of oppressive governments being muzzled forcing them to remain silent.

Who will be the emergent leaders that will stand up against this oppression? Who will speak for the voiceless? Who will shine a light into dark spaces exposing the truth of oppression? Who will shout, "Freedom!" to the millions who are captive? If we wish to be such a voice let's learn from the stories of those who have been or currently are voices of freedom in communities of injustice.

21Wilberforce has had the burden of traveling to places where we have heard stories of atrocities committed against children, women, and men because of their religion and belief. When we were in Nigeria, parents wept while telling us of the kidnapping of their daughters by Boko Haram. In Iraq young women who escaped from ISIS described to us the humiliating practices they experienced and the physical abuse and torture of the girls that were left behind. Again in Nigeria, village leaders told us of Fulani militants who came into their community at night killing villagers and burning their houses and churches to the ground. We have interviewed survivors of prisons in China, North Korea, Eretria, Turkey, and other oppressive governments. We have developed friendships and partnerships with folks who have been beaten, tortured, raped, and abused in horrific ways.

The only way to describe what we have seen and heard is their actions are the personification of the depravity of evil. However, as we began to judge these folks with self-righteous indignation, God continues to reveal to us our own greed when others have so little, our apathy when others are humiliated, and our racism that tolerates and even supports oppression. We cannot deny the truth of Scripture: "Then the Lord saw that the wickedness of man was great on the earth, and that every intent of the thoughts of his heart was only evil continually" (Genesis 6:5); and again, "For all have sinned and fall short of the glory of God" (Romans 3:23).

Just as God sent Moses to free the Hebrews from slavery to the Egyptians, God sent His own Son, Jesus, to liberate us from our bondage to sin. "For He rescued us from the domain of darkness, and transferred us to the kingdom of His beloved Son, in whom we have redemption, the forgiveness of sins" (Colossians 1:13-14).

The two primary events of Scripture are the Exodus and the cross. Both have to do with freedom from bondage.

Paul writes of our slavery to sin resulting in death or slavery to obedience to God resulting in righteousness (Romans 6:16-17). Paul himself had been a slave to legalism until Jesus brought spiritual transformation to him that opened his eyes to the freedom given to him through God's grace. Even though Paul was a prisoner when he wrote the letter to the church at Philippi, he speaks of joy and rejoicing.

When women and men see themselves as created in the image of God, they begin to see others also as persons of value. William Wilberforce had a spiritual transformation. His eyes were opened to the evil of slavery and he spent his adult life working for their freedom. Martin Luther King, Jr. gave his life to bring freedom for Blacks in America who were suffering from Jim Crow laws and other repressive practices of discrimination.

Some transformational leaders operate on a grand stage while others may lead a church, a company, an institution, or local government to find freedom from unproductive or unjust practices.

The year 2020 has been a challenging and painful one. The pandemic, social unrest, wars, religious persecution, economic collapse, and natural disasters have brought unprecedented suffering. The post-pandemic reality will require new paradigms in almost every arena of life. Who will be the *emergent leaders* that will challenge repressive and ineffective systems? Failure to recognize the seismic shifts confronting both our local and global communities in 2020 will be as reckless as Lewis and Clark who expected to find a waterway that would take them to the Pacific Ocean when they reached the Missouri River, but instead found the Rocky Mountains. They certainly didn't need better canoes to navigate the mountains.[2]

Emergent leaders are visionary, risk-takers, passionate, creative, and courageous. The response to the challenges of 2020 requires leaders who will guide churches, non-profits, schools, small businesses, governments, and every area of society to find opportunities to oppose unfair laws, ineffective systems and repressive practices.

On May 4, 1961, John Lewis and twelve other young riders including seven blacks and six whites, boarded Greyhound and Trailways buses with the plan to travel through Virginia, the Carolinas, Georgia, Alabama, and Mississippi, ending in New Orleans where a civil rights rally was planned. The *Freedom Riders* protested the Jim Crow segregation practices across the South to test an earlier Supreme Court ruling that banned racial discrimination in interstate travel. They were joined by others along the route and were met with unbelievable violence, brutality, attempted murders, and false imprisonment. Yet these Freedom Riders courageously continued to call attention to these racist practices and brought international attention to unjust laws that were ultimately overturned.

The suffering resulting from the trials of 2020 offers a window of opportunity to freedom leaders who will seize the moment, assess the challenges, learn from the past, and explore new options for unlocking the shackles that confine us. What is the one thing that burdens you the most: unjust laws, suffering children, religious persecution, hunger, declining churches, homelessness, sex trafficking, or unemployment? Are you willing to pay the price to become equipped to become a transformational leader that addresses your burden? If so, you will need like-minded partners, perseverance, and courage.

This book, *Speak Freedom*, will not provide you with the passion and heart you will need to bring sustainable social change; only God can give you that. However, my prayer is you will find some tools in this book that will assist you to pursue a journey that will offer freedom to those shackled to ineffective or oppressive systems that imperil the vulnerable.

1 Transformation Precedes Passion

"And do not be conformed to this world, but be transformed by the renewing of your mind, so that you may prove what the will of God is, that which is good and acceptable and perfect" (Romans 12:2).

On May 14, 1784, Wilberforce took his seat for the county of York, the most influential post in the British Parliament. "William Wilberforce had, at twenty-four, the most coveted seat in all of Parliament. He seemed unstoppable. With his extraordinary eloquence, brilliance, and charm—and with the prime minister as his dearest friend—there seemed no end in sight to where he might rise."[3] Wilberforce had all of the things most people covet: money, prestige, entertainment, and influential friends. "He did most of what everyone else did—he danced, and sang and spent countless hours indulging in the endless meals that were then the fashion of high society.[4] No one could have ever imagined that this self-indulgent son of privilege and opportunity would become the champion of slaves.

In 1785, when Wilberforce was twenty-six he experienced what he called the Great Change. God opened his eyes to a world of compassion, grace and righteousness. The change was not all of a sudden. It seldom is. God brought key people into William's life long before his awakening. A spiritual revival was already taking place throughout England and even in the colonies. Fifty years earlier three young men came to Oxford University in the 1730's that God would use to awaken two continents. Two of the men, John and Charles Wesley were brothers. They started a group that was dubbed the Holy Club and were mocked by others who called them Methodists because of their methodical use of time.

The third person was George Whitfield who later had an impact throughout England but was also the primary influence for the Great Awakening in North America. He preached almost 20,000 times to an estimated 10 million listeners throughout Great Britain and the American colonies. Some have said 80% of the people living in the colonies from Maine to Georgia heard him speak. His methods were controversial and he was unwelcomed among the clergy so he went directly to the people preaching in open fields to crowds numbering among the tens of thousands. Whitfield preached a gospel of inclusion for men, women, blacks, whites, and American Indians. Benjamin Franklin came to hear him as a skeptic but became one of Whitfield's strongest supporters.

"Whitfield was despised by the Church of England. But the press and those opposed to religion hated him too. He didn't mince words on the subjects of sin and hell, and he was increasingly impossible to avoid as his fame grew and grew."[5]

God used a tragedy in Wilberforce's childhood to expose him to the teaching of Whitfield and the Wesley's. His oldest sister died when she was only fourteen. Shortly after her death his mom had another baby, her fourth child. Unexpectedly four months later his father died at the age of forty. This was all too much for Wilberforce's mother and when she became ill with a fever she sent the ten-year-old Billy, as he was known at that time, to live with his Uncle William and Aunt Hannah in Wimbledon. His new guardians were extremely wealthy and Uncle William's brother-in-law was John Thornton, one of the wealthiest men in all of England.

Wilberforce's mother might have never sent him to live with them if she had known they were "Methodists." While she and her family were Christians by heritage, religion had its place. Respectable families needed to relegate religion to its own corner and not allow it to spill over into excesses as emotional Methodists were experiencing. Demonstrative religion was not a part of the ambitious dreams William's mother had for him.

Yet God had other plans for Wilberforce. The Wesley brothers and Whitfield were close friends of Uncle William and Aunt Hannah. Even though it was improbable that Wilberforce ever met Whitfield who left for his final trip to America about the time William came to live with his relatives, Whitfield's influence on William and Hannah was passed along to ten year old William. In addition to the three famous evangelists, Wilberforce was also introduced to his guardians' friend John Newton, who called himself "the Old African Blasphemer," because of his past as a slave ship captain before his own conversion. Billy undoubtedly heard Newton expound on the evils of slavery, as he was the parson of a nearby church in Olney.

When William's mother learned of the influence of Methodism on her young son she quickly brought him home to protect him from such foolishness. Immediately she began to free him from the indoctrination he received the two previous years. By the time Wilberforce became a young Member of Parliament, he had rejected the faith of his aunt and uncle and often even ridiculed it. In his new position of fame and prestige Wilberforce had more engaging issues to command his attentions. And yet God was still at work in his life and would bring other significant individuals to reveal to him the power of the gospel.

After Wilberforce had been elected to the most prestigious seat in Parliament, he decided to spend the winter on the French and Italian Riviera with his sister Sally, his mother, and their cousin Bessie Smith. Sally, whose actual name was Sarah, and William were the only two children from the four born to their mother who survived to adulthood.

Isaac Milner, the famous academic who was a tutor at Queens College, Cambridge, also joined them. Eric Metaxas describes Milner as "Stephen Hawking, Dick Cavett, and Andre the Giant all rolled into one."[6] Milner was literally a giant mentally and physically. It must have been a sight seeing Milner and Wilberforce together since Wilberforce was only about five foot three and weighed little more than a hundred pounds.

When they were ready to depart for their trip, William saw a book his cousin, Bessie Smith brought entitled, *The Rise and Progress of Religion in the Soul*, by Philip Doddridge. He asked Milner his opinion of the book and Milner said, "It is one of the best books ever written." They decided to discuss the book on their journey. The conversations about the Doddridge book later led to study of the Greek New Testament and discussions about theology.

Outwardly Wilberforce appeared unchanged; yet he was undergoing a transformation of heart. In his diary he wrote, "What madness is the course I am pursuing. I believe all the great truths of the Christian religion, but I am not acting as though I did. Should I die in this state I must go into a place of misery."[7] "In a letter to his friend Lord Muncaster, he despairs over the entrenched selfishness he saw among the rich and privileged, who behaved, in his view, like drunken parents who have abandoned their dying children."[8]

Wilberforce was experiencing a great turmoil of the soul. God was opening his eyes to the injustices of the world and convicting him of his silent and complicit involvement. His sullen behavior caused some to believe he was having a breakdown. He was filled with guilt and awareness that he must declare himself to the world and not deny Christ. He wrote, "I must awake to my dangerous state, and never be at rest till I have made my peace with God. My heart is so hard, my blindness so great, that I cannot get a due hatred of sin, though I see I am all corrupt, and blinded to the perception of spiritual things."[9]

Three days later, his journey led him back to his old friend John Newton whom he had not seen since he was a boy. He expected Newton to say he must abandon politics. However, Newton surprised him by telling him to stay in Parliament and that God will use him there. Afterward Wilberforce writes, "When I came away I found my mind in a calm, tranquil state, more humbled, and looking more devoutly up to God."[10]

Before Wilberforce could bring peace to the slaves he had to find his own personal peace with God. Transformational leaders must first experience a personal transformation. How could Wilberforce ever notice the horrors of slavery when he accommodated his own slavery to self-centeredness and the culture of his day? Only after God's conviction and Wilberforce's brokenness, confession and yielding to God's plan for his life, was he able to see slaves as individuals of worth and value created in the image and likeness of God. The persuasion of the world was no match to the persistent urging of the Holy Spirit and William Wilberforce submitted himself fully to following Christ.

The conversion of the Apostle Paul appears much more sudden than the agonizing journey of Wilberforce. In an instant a blinding light flashed around Saul, and a voice from Heaven called out, "'Saul, Saul, why are you persecuting Me?' And he said, 'Who are You, Lord?' And He said, 'I am Jesus whom you are persecuting, but get up and enter the city, and it will be told you what you must do'" (Acts 9:4-6). God led Saul to Damascus where he met Ananias who laid hands on him and said, "Brother Saul, the Lord Jesus, who appeared to you on the road by which you were coming, has sent me so that you may regain your sight and be filled with the Holy Spirit" (Acts 9:17). Saul, who was blinded by the light, was healed, filled with the Holy Spirit, and was baptized. Saul lost his physical sight temporarily so he would see the light of Christ. Saul the persecutor became Paul, the disciple of Christ.

Even though Paul's transformation was abrupt, God was working in his life all along. Paul was a devout Jew and seeking to earn the favor of God through his heritage and good works. "If anyone else has a mind to put confidence in the flesh, I far more: circumcised the eighth day, of the nation of Israel, of the tribe of Benjamin, a Hebrew of Hebrews; as to the Law, a Pharisee; as to zeal, a persecutor of the church; as to the righteousness which is in the Law, found blameless. But whatever things were gain to me, those things I have counted as loss for the sake of Christ. More than that, I count all things to be loss in view of the surpassing value of knowing Christ Jesus my Lord, for whom I have suffered the loss of all things, and count them but rubbish so that I may gain Christ" (Philippians 3:4-8).

Paul thought he was serving God through his life of morality. Even in his acts of persecution of the Christians, his motivation was driven by his sense of loyalty to God. Yet while still in his life of rebellion, God was working in his life. The same Scripture Paul used to justify his actions against the Church enlightened his path once his spiritual eyes were opened. Paul's nature of self-righteousness had to be broken down before he recognized his own depravity and dependence upon God. The religious zealot became the greatest evangelist to the Gentiles, who were once the very ones despised by the proud Jew.

Emergent leadership is hard work. Transformational leaders face opposition from those whose positions are threatened by individuals challenging unjust systems. The Apostle Paul endured flogging, beatings, prison, and ultimately execution for his new cause. These were in addition to the natural hardships of his journey including shipwrecks, hunger, thirst, criticism, loneliness, and rejection. William Wilberforce didn't undergo the magnitude of Paul's physical suffering but certainly knew criticism, loss of friends and allies, and felt the constant sting of the agony of one who internalizes the cruel sufferings of others.

The discouragement of facing the lies of those who benefitted from the profits of slavery was persistent throughout his life. Wilberforce must have been tempted to quit the fight on behalf of slaves when anticipated legislative victories became unexpected defeats. His enemies never gave up. The forces of evil appeared well funded with greater resources than those who stood for justice. Wilberforce even knew the sting of betrayal of those who professed support for his cause only to betray him when Parliamentary votes were taken.

The war against slavery wasn't a *sprint* but a *marathon* that continued until slavery was finally abolished in Britain just three days before his death. Some great heroes of faith never see the victory including those mentioned in Hebrews 11 who did not experience what was promised (Hebrews 11:39).

Emergent leadership is not for the faint hearted. Divine strength is required for those who wish to battle evil. Unjust systems and oppression of the righteous are never easily eradicated. However, we know from the promises of Scripture that there will be a day when justice is realized. "For our struggle is not against flesh and blood, but against the rulers, against the powers, against the world forces of this darkness, against the spiritual forces of wickedness in the heavenly places" (Ephesians 6:12). Leaders will need to fortify themselves daily with spiritual armor, pray without ceasing, express gratitude for small victories and never forget we are not alone in this struggle. "What does the Lord require of you but to do justice, to love kindness, and to walk humbly with your God?" (Micah 6:8).

Several of us from 21Wilberforce traveled to Iraq in January of 2015, to see for ourselves the genocide that ISIS declared against Christians and other religious minorities. We witnessed the devastation of thousands of families driven from their homes in the Nineveh Plains to an unsettled destination. The families were given three options: convert to Islam, be killed, or flee. Churches had flourished in this region since the first century. Families lived there for generations. In December of 2014, in their homeland, church bells failed to ring out for the first time since the first century because the Christians had been driven out of the region. Abruptly, they left everything: their houses, businesses, farms, churches, schools, and all of their possessions with no hope for restoration.

We interviewed hundreds of them and heard heart-breaking stories. A few years later ISIS was driven from the area, yet most refugees have still been unable to return. In the summer of 2019, I heard Archbishop Nicodemus of the Orthodox Church describe being driven from Mosul where he served. He spoke at a meeting hosted by the United States State Department before diplomats from over 100 countries saying, "ISIS took away our land. ISIS took away our homes. ISIS took away dignity. But ISIS can never take Jesus from our heart."

Paul wrote to suffering Christians in Rome, as well as Christians throughout the ages, reminding us that the struggles and suffering we may experience fail to compare to the glory that is to be revealed to us. "For I consider that the sufferings of this present time are not worthy to be compared with the glory that is to be revealed to us" (Romans 8:18). The battle continues but the victory is assured.

Endnotes

[1] Clayborne Carson, Editor, *The Autobiography of Martin Luther King*, Jr. (New York, NY: Warner Books, 1998), 207.

[2] This illustration is the basis for *Canoeing the Mountains* by Tod Bolsinger (Downers Grove, IL: IVP Books, 2015).

[3] Eric Metaxas, Amazing Grace (New York, NY: HarperCollins, 2007), 42.

[4] Ibid., 52

[5] Ibid., 8.

[6] Ibid., 51.

[7] Ibid., 53.

[8] Ibid.

[9] Ibid., 55.

[10] Ibid., 60.

2
The Power of Purpose

"'For I know the plans that I have for you,' declares the Lord, 'plans for welfare and not for calamity to give you a future and a hope. Then you will call upon Me and come and pray to Me, and I will listen to you. You will seek Me and find Me when you search for Me with all your heart'" (Jeremiah 29:11-13).

On August 31, 2020, Jim Denison spoke of the power of purpose in his cultural commentary, *The Daily Article*.

> "Chadwick Boseman, the actor who played the title character in the Oscar-winning film Black Panther, died last Friday at the age of forty-three. Boseman had previously drawn accolades for his depictions of Thurgood Marshall, Jackie Robinson, and James Brown. He died on the fifty-seventh anniversary of the March on Washington and the day baseball honored Jackie Robinson....
>
> Chadwick Boseman died of cancer, but he died in faith....
>
> In explaining Jackie Robinson's remarkable courage, Boseman quoted the fruit of the Spirit (Galatians 5:22-23), and

> said, 'I feel like it's because he had God in him that he was able to make it through this.'...
>
> Denison continues, "In his 2018 commencement address at his alma mater, Howard University, Bozeman quoted Jeremiah 29:11, which states, 'I know the plans I have for you, declares the Lord, plans for welfare and not for evil, to give you a future and a hope.'
>
> He then said, 'Graduating class, hear me well on this day... You would rather find purpose than a job or career. Purpose crosses disciplines. Purpose is an essential element of you. It is the reason you are on the planet at this particular time in history...The struggles along the way are only meant to shape you for your purpose.' He added: 'When God has something for you, it doesn't matter who stands against it. God will move someone who is holding you back away from a door and put someone there who will open it for you if it's meant for you...If you are willing to take the harder way, the more complicated one, the one with more failures at first than successes, the one that has ultimately proven to have more meaning, more victory, more glory, then you will not regret it.' Chadwick Boseman's death came too soon. But not before he discovered his purpose in life."[1]

Becoming an *emergent leader* is not the result of a burning desire for personal greatness; but a recognition that God has a plan for your life, and worldly accomplishments will never fill the hunger in your soul to live for the purpose for which you have been created.

A few years ago, I met Anglican Archbishop Ben Kwashi and his wife Dr. Gloria Kwashi in Jos, Nigeria. Our team had just spent a week in the Middle Belt of Nigeria where we saw villages that were burned to the ground, and interviewed hundreds of victims of religious violence. We entered IDP (Internally Displaced People) camps where thousands were crowded into tents after being driven from their homes. They told us stories of women and children murdered in their own beds by radical terrorists who came with AK-47 rifles and swords killing or evicting families from their own homes.

We heard stories about Bishop Kwashi and his wife. They too had suffered greatly and barely escaped death. Yet they continued to be a voice against injustice and literally took into their home children orphaned by violence, some who were living in the streets. I presupposed from the title (Archbishop) Kwashi would be austere, grim, and private, hardened by persecution. I could not have been more wrong. Ben and Gloria greeted us with broad smiles full of the joy of the Lord. We met them in a restaurant and then went to their house where we met the 67 children they had adopted. I watched them interact with the children and amazingly saw the smiles and cheers from kids from the ages of 1-15 who had been abandoned. Ben took his shepherd's rod and played it like an air guitar. The children screamed in delight. Then they sang to us "Jesus Loves Me" in English.

Gloria was born in 1958 in Lamurde in the northeast of Nigeria. Her father was the Crown Prince of the town of Rugange in Adamawa; thus Gloria was known as a princess. Her grandfather had been the first colonially installed king in 1946. She came from a Lutheran family and after secondary school gained admission to the interdenominational Theological College of Northern Nigeria. There she met Ben who was in his third year at the college.

Gloria, as only one of two girls at the college, received plenty of attention. Initially, Ben was not one of the ones reaching out to her. Ben wrote, "She was not my type. Gloria was a typical country girl who really didn't want to be noticed, a simple village girl who was so naïve she didn't even know how to make herself up. At least theological college ought to be a safe place for a country girl like this."[2] Gloria was equally unimpressed with Ben. She was obviously critical of him when she told one of Ben's friends, "Look at this Lagos chap! He's dressed for a party!"[3]

Ben and Gloria met in 1980 and in spite of their early differences and rocky few years of courtship and struggles, Gloria finally agreed to marry Ben in 1983. Together they served in a variety of rural and urban churches before moving to Jos in 1992, when her husband was consecrated and installed as the third Bishop of the Diocese of Jos.

Gloria and Ben are no strangers to persecution: as a young couple, their vicarage and church were burned down in 1987; in Jos they survived horrendous attacks from hired assassins. Ben was away at a meeting in London, February 2006. Gloria and her children were home. Thirty minutes after Ben had a phone conversation with Gloria, he received a call from his terrified daughter Hannatu. "Daddy, Daddy, they are armed! There are many of them. Please, Daddy, don't let anything happen to Mummy. Help her!"[4]

Ben got on his knees beside the bed and prayed for Gloria and the children. "'Please spare the children, spare Gloria.' If only I could have been in Jos at that moment. I was desperate and angry. I was asking God to do some miracle, to rescue Gloria and the children. I cried for them all, 'Lord, show Your power, show Your greatness, blind the killers, may they never get in.'"[5]

God did spare the lives of Gloria and the children, but they were horribly brutalized. Gloria was left temporarily blind, with broken bones, humiliated and tortured by her attackers; but to the glory of God their ministry has not been weakened. To the contrary of what might have been expected, their dedication has grown from strength to strength.

Gloria has a passion for working with women and children. As a young pastor's wife, she began the Girls' Guild, which has now spread over many dioceses. For over 25 years, she has been Diocesan President of the Mothers' Union, Women's Guild, and Girls' Guild, and is also the Provincial Trainer for the Mothers' Union (Church of Nigeria). She is an experienced teacher and has led many retreats, particularly for pastors' and bishops' wives.

Her deep concern for orphans and vulnerable children has grown to such an extent that she and her husband now have adopted dozens of children who are living with them in their house. She has also begun the Zambiri Outreach and Child Care Centre, with a school which has now grown into a primary and secondary school with over 400 pupils—all of whom receive free education, free feeding, uniforms, and medical care. This is transforming the lives of the pupils, of families, and of the community.

Since that first night, Ben and Gloria have become our good friends. I continue to be inspired by their joy, peace, and righteousness. They tirelessly challenge injustice. Persecution and the threat of death hover over them. They are not exempt from the challenges of raising children from difficult backgrounds, shepherding churches, raising funds, church conflict, and Covid-19. Ben and Gloria have their good days and difficult days. Yet they appear to me to be earthly vessels filled with the righteousness of God's Spirit.

On the back cover of his biography, *Neither Bomb nor Bullet*, by Andrew Boyd, Ben makes a statement that summarizes his priorities, "Until my time is up, I will live each moment for the gospel, which is the hope of Africa and the world."[6]

God clearly showed the Apostle Paul his life's purpose upon Paul's conversion. The Lord said to Ananias, "Go, for he [Paul] is a chosen instrument of Mine, to bear My name before the Gentiles and kings and the sons of Israel; for I will show him how much he must suffer for My name's sake" (Acts 9:15-16). Paul's understanding of the clear purpose for his life brought courage to him during times of great difficulties. He never forgot that God rescued him from the slavery of self-righteousness and freed him to experience the joy of God's righteousness.

Paul wrote to the Christians in Rome of this new freedom. "Knowing this, that our old self was crucified with Him, in order that our body of sin might be done away with, so that we would no longer be slaves to sin; for he who has died is freed from sin" (Romans 6:6-7). "Do you not know that when you present yourselves to someone as slaves for obedience, you are slaves of the one whom you obey, either of sin resulting in death, or of obedience resulting in righteousness? But thanks be to God that though you were slaves of sin, you became obedient from the heart to that form of teaching to which you were committed, and having been freed from sin, you became slaves of righteousness" (Romans 6:16-18).

William Wilberforce began to understand his life's purpose when he was a young Member of Parliament and spent the rest of his life pursuing the fulfillment of his calling. However, unlike Wilberforce, some experience God's purpose for their lives when they are older, as did Moses who was 80 years old when God called him to set His Hebrew people free from their bondage as slaves in Egypt.

I recently met Mrs. Goo[7] when I was in South Korea. She escaped from North Korea and at the age of 83 is now a missionary to other North Koreans wherever they may be living.

Mrs. Goo was born in 1937 in a Christian home in North Korea. They had a Bible in her household and a framed script on the wall that said, "Christ is Lord of this house." Her parents prayed she would be a servant of the Lord and she grew up dreaming she would be an evangelist. Her father was a successful mine owner and her mother ran a pharmacy out of their home. Both parents used their positions to help the poor.

This was before August 15, 1945, when Korea was liberated from Japan and they were divided into two nations. The Communist Party was strong in the North and many Christians fled to the South including their pastor. Her parents sent three of her brothers to the south to earn a living, but she and the rest of her family stayed and her father became the pastor of their congregation.

In the mid-60's, a religious group came to her brother's house to lead worship and her brother burned a picture of Kim Il-Sung, because he said it was an idol. One of the members in the group snitched and her brother was arrested and sentenced to 20 years in prison—he didn't survive. Her parents were relocated to work in a mine. Her husband was forced to divorce her because members of his family were high-ranking communist officials. She was deprived of her two children who were 3 years old and 8 months old and would never see them again.

Later she was forced to marry a man who had been a teacher in China who had eight children. The agony of having to raise eight children from another woman while being separated from her own led to great anguish and to thoughts of suicide. Yet God kindled in her a love for those children and blessed her with two more children with this husband.

She endured great hardships, but by the grace of God she was able to escape to South Korea where she worked as a domestic laborer until her youngest child was old enough to be married. She enrolled in an underground missionary training school and when she graduated she became a missionary at the age of 82.

Mrs. Goo said, "My life has been marked by great suffering because I carry the name of Jesus. But it has also been marked by even greater grace, because Christ brings good out of whatever the enemy intends for evil."

God answered her father's prayer for her life and Mrs. Goo is now an evangelist at 83 years of age. None of us is too old to experience God's call. Has God given you a burden to stand against an injustice in your community?

Endnotes

[1] On August 31, 2020, Jim Denison wrote of the power of purpose in his cultural commentary, *The Daily Article.*

[2] Andrew Boyd, *Neither Bomb nor Bullet,* (Oxford, England: Lion Hudson, 2019), 74-75.

[3] Ibid., 75.

[4] Ibid., 202.

[5] Ibid., 203.

[6] Ibid., back cover.

[7] Her name was changed for her protectiown.

3
A God-Given Burden

"When I heard these words, I sat down and wept and mourned for days; and I was fasting and praying before the God of heaven" (Nehemiah 1:4).

Although Nehemiah held a position of honor, cupbearer to the king, he never forgot the conditions of his native city of Jerusalem. He was one of the exiled Jews who had risen to power among the Persian administration of King Artaxerxes. Nehemiah was in the spring residence of the king in Susa, the capital, when his brother Hanani came to him from Judah. He asked his brother and some of the men from Judah who came with him, "concerning the Jews who had escaped and had survived the captivity and about Jerusalem. They said to me, 'The remnant there in the province who survived the captivity are in great distress and reproach, and the wall of Jerusalem is broken down and its gates are burned with fire'" (Nehemiah 1:2-3).

The glory days of Jerusalem were a distant past. King David had towered over other kings and when his son, Solomon, was king, the Queen of Sheba described her visit to Jerusalem, "It was a true report which I heard in my own land about your words and your wisdom. Nevertheless I did not believe the reports, until I came and my eyes had seen it. And behold, the half was not told me. You exceed in wisdom and prosperity the report which I heard" (1 Kings 10:6-7).

Hanani's report confirmed that the glory of Israel had departed. The land was in shambles and the people were without leadership and complacent about the devastation.

When Nehemiah heard these words he was crushed and sat down and wept and mourned for days, fasting and praying to the Lord. "I beseech You, O Lord God of heaven, the great and awesome God, who preserves the covenant and lovingkindness for those who love Him and keep His commandments, let Your ear now be attentive and Your eyes open to hear the prayer of Your servant which I am praying before You now, day and night, on behalf of the sons of Israel Your servants, confessing the sins of the sons of Israel which we have sinned against You; I and my father's house have sinned" (Nehemiah 1:5-6).

For four months, Nehemiah was distressed and continually prayed and wept over the condition of his homeland. He turned to God's Word and was reminded of God's promises as well as His warnings. Nehemiah could have put the burden for Jerusalem out of his own mind with the justification that he should not be concerned if his kinsmen who lived in Jerusalem were apathetic. After all, life was pretty good for him living in the comfort of the king's presence.

Why were the inhabitants of Jerusalem complacent about the situation? They obviously observed the eroded conditions of the city daily. Was there no leader left in Judah to stir up the people to remedy the problem? Were they content to be the laughing-stock of other nations and allow the name of God to be slandered among others? Where was their pride and sense of justice?

The silence of good people enables injustice to reign. The people in Wilberforce's day were unbothered by the atrocities of slavery. What concern were the slaves for the folks in London? They had their own problems caring for their families, finding jobs, and trying to make ends meet. Besides, slavery had been around forever and it was an essential part of the economy. The stories of slaves being better off in their new conditions rather than the poverty of their native lands were enough to calm the conscience of the ones who may have been tempted to worry about slavery. Not until Wilberforce and other abolitionists placed the horrors of slavery right in front of the people were their hearts stirred. Wilberforce said, "You may choose to look the other way, but no longer can you say I didn't know."

Emergent leaders must become burdened about injustice before they are willing to pay the price to bring about change. Nehemiah knew he was risking his own position and perhaps even his own life if he brought his problems before the king. Why should the king be bothered about the concerns of his cupbearer? Yet Nehemiah was prepared to respond when the king asked about his sadness. Nehemiah said, "Let the king live forever. Why should my face not be sad when the city, the place of my fathers' tombs, lies desolate and its gates have been consumed by fire?" (Nehemiah 2:3). Then when asked, Nehemiah set out the plan he had already formulated in his mind and placed it before the king.

Jesus' love for broken humanity compelled Him to redeem us from our bondage to sin. "Although He existed in the form of God, did not regard equality with God a thing to be grasped, but emptied Himself, taking the form of a bond-servant, and being made in the likeness of men. Being found in the appearance as a man, He humbled Himself by becoming obedient to the point of death, even death on a cross" (Philippians 2:6-8). The multitudes Jesus fed and healed and who had seen Jesus raise the dead, would have gladly made Him king. Yet Jesus never forgot the price of redemption. "Just as the Son of Man did not come to be served, but to serve, and to give His life a ransom for many" (Matthew 20:28).

On August 28, 1963, Martin Luther King, Jr. stood before a crowd of nearly 250,000 people, consisting of dignitaries, celebrities, and a mass of ordinary people, some who already had suffered from the brutality of those in power. With the statue of Lincoln behind him, King challenged the eager crowd with a message that changed history.

> "Five score years ago, a great American, in whose symbolic shadow we stand today, signed the Emancipation Proclamation. This momentous decree came as a great beacon of light of hope to millions of Negro slaves, who had been seared in the flames of withering injustice. It came as a joyous daybreak to end the long night of their captivity.
>
> But one hundred years later, the Negro still is not free. One hundred years later, the life of the Negro is still sadly crippled by the manacles of segregation and the chains of discrimination. One hundred years later, the Negro lives on a lonely island of poverty in the midst of a vast ocean of material prosperity. One hundred years later, the Negro is still languished in the corners of American society and finds himself an exile in his own land. And so we've come here today to dramatize a shameful condition.

In a sense, we've come to our nation's capital to cash a check. When the architects of our republic wrote the magnificent words of the Constitution and the Declaration of Independence, they were signing a promissory note to which every American was to fall heir. This note was a promise that all men, yes, black men as well as white men, would be guaranteed the unalienable rights of 'Life, Liberty, and the pursuit of Happiness.'...

It would be fatal for the nation to overlook the urgency of the moment. This sweltering summer of the Negro's legitimate discontent will not pass until there is an invigorating autumn of freedom and equality. Nineteen sixty-three is not an end, but a beginning. And those who hope that the Negro needed to blow off steam and will now be content will have a rude awakening if the nation returns to business as usual...

We cannot be satisfied as long as a Negro in Mississippi cannot vote and a Negro in New York believes he has nothing for which to vote. No, no, we are not satisfied and we will not be satisfied until justice rolls down like waters and righteousness like a mighty stream...

I have a dream that my four little children will one day live in a nation where they will not be judged by the color of their skin but by the content of their character...

I have a dream that one day every valley shall be exalted, every hill and mountain shall be made low, the rough places will be made plain and the crooked places will be made straight and the glory of the Lord shall be revealed and all flesh shall see it together...

> And when this happens, when we allow freedom to ring, when we let it ring from every village and every hamlet, from every state and every city, we will be able to speed up that day when all of God's children, black men and white men, Jews and Gentiles, Protestants and Catholics, will be able to join hands and sing in the words of the old Negro spiritual, 'Free at last, free at last. Thank God Almighty, we are free at last.'"[1]

For one hundred years after the Emancipation Proclamation, there were still two Americas. Even to this day injustice is tolerated. Blacks are often forced to live in segregated neighborhoods with inadequate streets, housing, schools, health care, and protection. For decades restrictions kept Blacks from the foundational American value of voting. All across the South, Blacks were forbidden to eat in restaurants with whites, had segregated water fountains, forced to the backs of buses, restricted from jobs because of the color of their skin, and treated with indignity.

In the mid-seventies, I was serving in my first full-time pastorate in a wonderful county seat town. The church had an incredible reputation as one of the leading churches in our state. The schools had integrated but the churches had not. One Sunday night two young Black boys came forward during our invitation and shared with the church they had made Jesus the boss of their lives. Our godly Deacon Chairman, Doc Jones, a prominent veterinarian in our town had led them to this decision. I'll never forget the joy of the moment. Unfortunately, it was short-lived. I called on one of my favorite deacons to lead us in the closing benediction and he offered a short prayer, "Father forgive us for what we have done. Amen."

I was stunned and hopeful that I misunderstood what he prayed. I was waiting for him when he arrived at his office the next morning anxious to ask about his prayer. He assured me that I had not misunderstood. He then shared with me his biblical beliefs that there should be no mixing of the races. Even though we continued to respect each other, we argued theology then and several times afterward without either of us convincing the other. Unfortunately, the responses from many in the congregation and even others outside of the church were even less conciliatory.

Our church was situated in the center of town just off the courthouse square, along with First Methodist Church and First Presbyterian Church. What happened in our churches didn't stay in our churches. The incident spilled over throughout the community and the crisis and rumors became abundant about Blacks coming to the town to stir up trouble. The situation became so tense that a special deacons' meeting was called to deal with the situation. Our deacon chairman asked us to get on our knees and pray; and we did for about thirty minutes. Afterward, he asked one of the men who was most upset about the "integration" of our church what was the problem. He answered with a vulgar statement of racism.

His comment opened the door of a spirited conversation about Blacks, Whites, and Browns worshiping together with both sides using Scripture to justify positions. The problem was not resolved that night but I was pleasingly shocked and encouraged that the vast majority of the deacons were praising God for the decisions the two young black boys made to follow Christ.

During those challenging days, I believed God was leading me to preach on the sin of racism. The church was packed and there was awkward feeling of tension. I confessed my own struggles with this issue and attempted to debunk biblical passages used by segregationists to justify the mistreatment of others according to race. We always ended our service with an opportunity to make public decisions. As soon as we began to sing the song of invitation the aisles were flooded with folks coming to the front of the church weeping and crying out to God to forgive them for their bigotry. The battle did not end that day but God used the courage of a godly deacon to stand up against injustice, forcing our church to confront our prejudice, and to begin moving toward a new attitude of compassion for all people.

A God-given burden for justice must precede meaningful change. *Emergent leaders face significant opposition anytime systemic change is considered.* Folks who have been empowered by structures that provide them power at the expense of others, will do whatever they can to protect their favored status. Martin Luther King, Jr., knew that opposition to segregation would be costly. After arrests, beatings, a stabbing, and other cruel assaults, on April 4, 1968, King was assassinated. Even though he had climbed to the top of the mountain and seen the other side where justice was available to all regardless of race, MLK knew he might not live to reach there himself.

A leader must understand the problem before she can recommend a solution. She must be broken, burdened, and determined enough to pay the price for transformative change. Systemic change doesn't come quickly or easily. Nehemiah, Wilberforce, and King faced an organized enemy who fought them each step of the way. Yet the writer of Hebrews was inspired by God who reminds us, "Fixing our eyes on Jesus, the author and perfecter of faith, who for the joy set before Him, endured the cross, despising the shame, and has sat down at the right hand of the throne of God" (Hebrews 12:2).

Endnotes

[1](Excerpts from King's speech, *The Autobiography of Martin Luther King, Jr.,* edited by Clayborne Carson, 223-227).

4
A Life of Passion

"I am telling the truth in Christ, I am not lying, my conscience testifies with me in the Holy Spirit, that I have great sorrow and unceasing grief in my heart. For I could wish that I myself were accursed, separated from Christ for the sake of my brethren, my kinsmen according to the flesh" (Romans 9:1-3).

Overthrowing unjust systems like racial discrimination or religious persecution requires more than an occasional letter to a Congressman or an Op Ed in a regional newspaper. While these can be part of a larger strategy, *transformation requires leaders who are passionate, fearless, and determined.*

In 2020, our nation celebrated the life of one such leader, Congressman John Lewis. Many of us will remember him as an elder statesman who was regarded as the conscience of Congress. However, his fight for justice began in much less prestigious circumstances. Lewis often told of his childhood experience preaching to the chickens behind his house, believing he was preparing himself to be a pastor when he may have been unknowingly practicing for speeches he would deliver on the floor of the U.S. House.

Lewis was committed to the civil rights movement even as a student at American Baptist College of Nashville, Tennessee, organizing desegregation of lunch counters in downtown Nashville. He led bus boycotts, voter rights, and other demonstrations for racial equality. He and his friends were dedicated to nonviolence, a discipline he practiced his entire life.

Lewis was one of the original Freedom Riders, seven Blacks and six Whites who rode from Washington, D.C., to New Orleans even though many of the southern states prohibited Black and White riders from sitting by each other on public transportation. He and the other Freedom Riders were beaten and arrested. Lewis, 21 years old, was the first who was assaulted while in Rock Hill, South Carolina. On another occasion, he was imprisoned for forty days in the Mississippi State Penitentiary after participating in a Freedom Riders activity. The Freedom Riders were beaten with baseball bats, lead pipes, chains, and stones. While in the Greyhound Bus Station in Montgomery, Lewis was hit with a wooden crate and left unconscious.

John Lewis became a public figure after his leadership role in the marches from Selma to Montgomery, when on Bloody Sunday, March 7, 1965, he and fellow activist Hosea Williams led over six hundred marchers across the Edmund Pettus Bridge in Selma. While the marchers were praying, the Alabama State Troopers charged them with tear gas and nightsticks. A blow to the head caused Lewis to suffer a skull fracture.

At 23 years of age, Lewis was the youngest of the "Big Six" who organized the 1963 March on Washington. In addition to Lewis and King, they included: Whitney Young, A. Philip Randolph, James Farmer, and Roy Wilkins. On August 28, John Lewis stood before a crowd of almost 250,000 and delivered his passionate speech just prior to the "I Have a Dream" speech of Martin Luther King, Jr.

Lewis began his speech, "We march today for jobs and freedom, but we have nothing to be proud of. For hundreds and thousands of our brothers and sisters are not here. For they are receiving starvation wages, or no wages at all. While we stand here, there are sharecroppers in the Delta of Mississippi who are out in the fields working for less than three dollars a day, twelve hours a day. While we stand here there are students in jail on trumped-up charges. Our brother James Farmer, along with many others, is also in jail. We come here today with a great sense of misgiving."

Lewis concluded with the challenge, "By the force of our demands, our determination, and our numbers, we shall splinter the segregated South into a thousand pieces and put them together in the image of God and democracy. We must say, 'Wake up America! Wake up!' For we cannot stop, and we will not and cannot be patient."[1]

John Lewis, Martin Luther King, Jr., and other civil rights leaders of the 1960's made an incredible impact overthrowing many of the Jim Crow laws and segregation practices of our nation. They paved the way for Black leaders to emerge in government, churches, medicine, business, sports, and practically every aspect of society. Lewis could have lived off his notoriety and sacrifice for the rest of his life. However, he knew what other transformational leaders know that the battle against evil is never complete in this life. He served in Congress for 17 terms, representing Georgia's 5th congressional district, where he continued to give passionate speeches and engage in "good trouble, necessary trouble," to achieve change.

Not all leaders serve on a national stage. Mr. Garrison was my sixth-grade teacher at the Greenbrier Elementary School in Fort Worth, Texas, who dedicated his life to helping children recognize their own worth and value. I was probably one of several students in the class who thought I was the teacher's pet. He found the time to let each of us know personally that we had great potential. He certainly didn't just work from 8:00–3:30. In addition to the planning, teaching, and grading tasks that consume hours each day, Mr. Garrison also coached our football and softball teams and worked with those of us who were patrol boys each day before and after class. Mr. Garrison is one of the reasons why I have always declared that my main heroes are nurses and teachers.

Effective leaders never bring about change by themselves. The battle for the abolition of slaves was not just the work of William Wilberforce, yet decades earlier others like the passionate and courageous Granville Sharp paved the way for the changing of the narrative among the public about the horrors of slavery through his speeches, writings, and judicial advocacy. On May 22, 1787, he chaired the newly formed Committee for the Abolition of the Slave Trade. He immediately began planning an extensive fact-finding mission to England's slave ports that summer.

> "His life would be threatened on numerous occasions in the months ahead, but the more he saw of the horrors of the slave trade, the more his zeal to end it increased. 'On whatever branch of the system I turned my eyes, I found it equally barbarous,' he wrote. 'The trade was, in short, one mass of iniquity from the beginning to the end.' ... Everywhere he turned there were fresh horrors. He climbed aboard slave ships and measured the spaces allotted for the slaves; he purchased the ghastliest implements of restraint

> and torture, from manacles and shackles to thumbscrews and branding irons. There was a device used to pry open the mouths of slaves who refused to eat. All he uncovered simply goaded him to uncover more."[2]

Thomas Clarkson, Sharp, and one other Anglican, Philip Sansom, joined with nine Quakers as founding members of a small non-denominational group, the Committee for the Abolition of Slavery. The Quakers were generally barred from the House of Commons until the early 19th century and the partnership with Anglicans helped them have access to lobby the Parliament. "One of the things that became quite clear to Clarkson and to Wilberforce was that the slave trade, like all evil systems, corrupted and ruined the lives of all who touched it."[3]

As early as the 18th century, abolitionists were attempting to outlaw slavery in America. By 1804, all Northern states, beginning with Pennsylvania in 1780, passed legislation abolishing slavery, although that did not always mean those already in slavery were freed. By 1790, all states banned international slave trade. Even though South Carolina joined in this action in 1787, it reversed itself in 1803. The Thirteenth Amendment to the U.S. Constitution made slavery unconstitutional in 1865.

One of the early Baptist leaders in the abolition movement was Virginia Baptist pastor Elder John Leland, who was one of the primary leaders who urged James Madison to include religious freedom in the U.S. Constitution. Baptist historian Fred Anderson wrote,

> "In the 18th century in Colonial Virginia there was only one church permitted by law—the Anglican Church, the Church of England which was the Established Church of Virgin-

> ia. Baptists were tolerated at times and in certain places but they were openly persecuted—beaten, whipped, imprisoned...Some forty Baptists, again primarily ministers, were imprisoned or otherwise severely persecuted. But we have also found an account of African slaves stripped and whipped for having dared to hear a Baptist minister preaching from his jail window...The people of the Established Church considered the Baptists to be the lowest of the low, the meanest of the mean...I believe the Africans felt at home within the Baptist churches of Virginia because they and the white Baptists shared the same social strata of those who were despised by the ruling class."[4]

When God entrusted the hope of heaven and the fear of hell to the Apostle Paul for him to deliver both to his own kinsmen as well as to Gentiles, Paul knew it required his whole commitment. Paul could not sit in Jerusalem and wait for those searching for truth to come to him. He set out on dangerous journeys to take the gospel to the people where they lived, whether they were religious leaders in the synagogues or philosophers at the Areopagus in Athens. These journeys and Paul's message of righteousness were threatening to corrupt leaders in places of power and often landed him in trouble.

Paul was beaten, stoned, put in prison, suffered from shipwrecks and ultimately executed. Yet Paul wrote, "To this present hour we are both hungry and thirsty, and are poorly clothed, and are roughly treated, and are homeless; and we toil, working with our own hands; when we are reviled, we bless; when we are persecuted, we endure; when we are slandered, we try to conciliate; we have become as the scum of the world, the dregs of all things, even until now" (1 Corinthians 4:11-13).

One might think Paul would have regretted that he left his life as a respected leader among his own people to suffer the hardship of persecution. However, in his short letter to the Philippians he wrote while still in prison, Paul uses the word "joy" or "rejoice" over twenty times illustrating his undaunted passion to share the gospel of Jesus.

> "But whatever things were gain to me, those things I have counted as loss for the sake of Christ. More than that, I count all things to be loss in view of the surpassing value of knowing Christ Jesus my Lord, for whom I have suffered the loss of all things, and count them but rubbish so that I may gain Christ, and may be found in Him, not having a righteousness of my own derived from the Law, but that which is through faith in Christ, the righteousness which comes from God on the basis of faith, that I may know Him and the power of His resurrection and the fellowship of His sufferings, being conformed to His death; in order that I may attain to the resurrection from the dead" (Philippians 3:7-11).

Preachers whose desire is to please hearers or members of Congress who spend their energies on party politics will never challenge injustice. Corrupt systems are torn down by passionate leaders who hate evil and love goodness; that value the lives of all and champion the cause of the voiceless. Each generation needs leaders like Gloria Kwashi, John Lewis, Granville Sharp, and Mr. Garrison, men and women who actually find their lives by giving them away. Perhaps God is calling you for such a noble task.

Endnotes

[1] (John Lewis, "Speech at the March on Washington" August 28, 1963).

[2] Metaxas, *Amazing Grace*, 116.

[3] Carson, *The Autobiography of Martin Luther King, Jr.*, 116.

[4] ("*Free Indeed*," Fred Anderson, Executive Director Virginia Baptist Historical Society on the 150th anniversary of emancipation, page 4.)

5 Clarifying Your Calling

"I press on so that I may lay hold of that for which I was laid hold of by Christ Jesus" (Philippians 3:12).

One of the most incredible men I have ever met was Pastor Dick Woodward of Williamsburg, Virginia. Dick was already a quadriplegic when I met him. I didn't know him when he was the popular founding pastor of the Virginia Beach Community Chapel for 25 years, or even when he served as pastor of the Williamsburg Community Chapel. The first time I met him he was already paralyzed, lying still on his bed, unable to move anything except his head. If a fly landed on his nose, he was unable to brush it away.

I had heard stories about this great man of faith. He gave bold leadership to each congregation he served. Dick was a popular local television pastor in the Hampton Roads area of Virginia. He was the founder of the Mini Bible College that taught Christian discipleship globally to make it easier for laypeople to understand the Bible. Even after he was completely paralyzed, because of a gift of a voice-activated computer, he continued to write his books.

I visited him to encourage him, yet the opposite happened. I learned from him that joy in the Lord had little to do with circumstances. His joy came from the power of God's Word and the indwelling of the Holy Spirit. Of course he wanted to be made well. He probably had gallons of oil poured over him by well-meaning Christians who prayed for his healing, yet that was obviously not God's plan for Dick.

I asked him about the secret of his life of victory and joy. He shared four insights. "I'm not but He is. I can't but He can. I don't want to, but He wants to. I didn't, but He did." After each statement Dick repeated, "And I am in Him and He is in me."

Dick Woodward would have never chosen his life as a quadriplegic if he had been given a choice. Of course that decision was not up to him, yet in that horrible tragedy he found the joy and the passion God provides for those who trust Him.

What is your life's ambition? What motivates you to get up every morning, to work when you would rather play, to prepare while others sit back? What is the driving force for your life? What a tragedy when a person has no ambition, focus, or dream; when he merely exists and moves along with the crowd. What is your Kingdom assignment?

The Apostle Paul was always reaching out to obtain what Christ Jesus already prepared for him. He knew his life wasn't controlled by unfortunate circumstances or by the wicked deeds of his enemies. Paul knew that even when tragedy came, God was still with him and had a plan for his life.

How can we find our Kingdom assignment? When I was a student in seminary one of my friends said he came to the conclusion that it was not God's will for him to work on a doctorate. I felt he made a wise decision because with his grade point he would not have been admitted to pursue such a program even with a letter from the Pope. I am 6’4” and weigh well over two hundred pounds, but I never prayed about whether I should become a professional football player or NBA basketball player. Those guys appear to have other qualities like speed, agility, and strength. Even though I think it would be fun to play on the PGA Seniors Tour, unfortunately I have difficulty scoring below the number on the thermometer on a hot Texas summer day.

As we seek God’s assignment for us, we should consider practical issues like interests, gifts, needs, resources, talents, and experiences. Today I received a text from an attorney friend in Houston who first described how busy his life was with demanding vocational challenges. However, he then said, “It’s been busy but I love this stuff.”

As a young boy I was always interested in politics. I thought I wanted to be an attorney because that appeared to be the primary vocation that led to holding office. From elementary school through college, I often ran for class officer, or even an office in other organizations to which I belonged, at times even successfully. When I was in high school I was on the debate team for all three years. From a young age I was fascinated with political conventions and continued to be until this year when by watching the virtual 2020 Democratic and Republican Conventions, I was cured of my obsession.

My original plans were sidetracked when I made a commitment as a senior in high school to a call to preach. For years I had begun to believe this might be the plan God had for my life. One Sunday afternoon I happened to read Ephesians 4:11-12 and I knew in my heart that God was calling me to preach. “And He gave some as apostles, and some as prophets, and some as evangelists, and some as pastors and teachers, for the equipping of the saints for the work of service, to the building up of the body of Christ." God confirmed for me that afternoon that He created me to be a pastor-teacher. That night at church I made my decision public. Afterward, some man I didn't even know stood up and said, "If God is calling him to preach I think we should let him preach next Sunday night." The church actually did let me preach and my text was the whole Bible and it took 18 minutes for me to say all that I knew about it.

If I had the decision to make over again I would always choose to be a pastor, a profession I have loved.

Little did I know that politics would still be a part of my life. I had the opportunity to be the Chaplain of the House of Representatives in Arkansas for four years while I was a pastor in Benton, Arkansas, because the Speaker of the House, Lacy Landers was a member of our church. Later, I had the privilege of being the pastor of Columbia Baptist Church in Falls Church, Virginia, near the nation's Capital. This opened fascinating doors to be involved with leaders in government. Later, I became a denominational executive and realized that politics in D.C. was tame compared to denominational politics.

In 1 Corinthians 12—14, the Bible speaks of the gifts of the Holy Spirit. All of Christ's followers are given spiritual gifts that are to be used to edify the Body of Christ. Just as there are many different members of a physical body, with all having different functions, so also there are many different gifts of the Spirit but the one Body of Christ. God has also gifted us with various talents. Why would He give us spiritual gifts and talents if they were not a part of His plan for our life? We are foolish to overlook the obvious interests, talents, and gifts that are ours when we seek to find God's plan for our lives.

The year 2020 has been full of global challenges. The Covid-19 virus was the first global pandemic since the 1918 influenza pandemic. In addition, there has been social unrest in our country and in different ways throughout the world. Economic shutdowns have brought rising unemployment and serious food and water shortages to large populations. Natural disasters like hurricanes, fires, and flooding bring even more grief to a world already in crisis. For many reasons, including the ever-present fear from the pandemic, social evils have been exposed shining a light on systemic injustice. Global religious persecution is at an all-time high. Community and global concerns create challenges that also provide opportunities for leaders to step up.

William Wilberforce and Granville Sharp found Kingdom assignments because the world tolerated the horrible practice of slavery. John Lewis and Martin Luther King, Jr. were motivated by the civil rights abuses of Blacks. When our son, Jeremy Everett recognized that thousands of children in Texas were hungry he, along with the help of others, founded the Texas Hunger Initiative (THI) that has expanded into the Baylor Collaborative on Hunger and Poverty. Jeremy and his team assumed there was plenty of food for all Texans but the problem was the distribution. They sought to answer the question, "How can Texans be assured that every child in the state has a nutritious meal every day?"

In just over a decade THI has created public private partnerships that have brought food to thousands of families. In 2019, they received a $5 million grant for a project to distribute food by mail to eligible students in rural communities during the summer months when school meals are not available. When this program was initiated, they did not know this opportunity provided them with a test case that led to the provision of meals to children in rural communities in over thirty states and Puerto Rico during the pandemic of 2020 when schools were closed.

The eleventh chapter of the book of Hebrews in the New Testament has been called God's Hall of Fame. The list contains individuals of fame and infamy like King David and a prostitute named Rahab. Abraham who was the father of nations and Moses the great emancipator were also included. The diverse list of people have one thing in common, they were all faithful to God's assignment for them even though most never saw the promise completely fulfilled in their lifetime. In the first verse of the next chapter of Hebrews we find, "Therefore, since we have so great a cloud of witnesses surrounding us, let us also lay aside every encumbrance and the sin which so easily entangles us, and let us run with endurance *the race that is before us*."[1]

God will not hold us responsible for the race that He sets before others, but for the one He has chosen for us. Even while Paul was chained and in prison he wrote, "I press on toward the goal for the prize of the upward call of God in Christ Jesus" (Philippians 3:14).

Discerning God's plan for your life is an ongoing process that encourages you even in the darkest moments and brings joy as you realize God is at work in you. "For I am confident of this very thing, that He who began a good work in you will perfect it until the day of Christ Jesus" (Philippians 1:6).

Do you know God's Kingdom assignment for you? Are you pursuing it with passion? Our greatest impact on society comes when we are in the center of God's will.

In the next section, we will study leaders who provide insights and models for those who desire to fulfill their Kingdom assignment with faithfulness, excellence, and effectiveness. Researchers have examined thousands of transformational leaders seeking to find common traits from the corporate world, faith communities, non-profits, government, and athletics that provide best practices for others. Gifted athletes may be born with natural abilities but only those who are disciplined to perfect their skills through preparation and hard work will achieve their best results. If athletes hone their skills through rigorous training, how much more should those who wish to bring justice where there is injustice commit themselves to running the race set before them with passion, competence, and endurance.

Endnotes

[1] Italics added

Part 2

Leading With Excellence: Learning Best Practices From Leaders Making an Impact

"Leadership is energizing a community of people toward their own transformation in order to accomplish a shared mission in the face of a changing world."[1]

James M. Kouzes and Barry Z. Posner wrote *The Leadership Challenge* based on decades of research in an attempt to identify best practices of excellent leadership. "Since 1983 we've been conducting research on personal-best leadership experiences, and we've discovered that there are countless examples of how leaders mobilize others to get extraordinary things done in virtually every arena of organized activity."[2] "As we looked deeper into the dynamic process of leadership, through case analyses and survey questionnaires, we uncovered five practices common to personal-best leadership experiences. When getting extraordinary things done in organizations, leaders engage these Five Practices of Exemplary Leadership:

- Model the Way
- Inspire a Shared Vision
- Challenge the Process
- Enable Others to Act
- Encourage the Heart"[3]

During the next few chapters, we will investigate how these practices have informed transformational leaders and how they are available to you, the reader. Before examining the best practices we must first learn effective tools to enable leaders to access the situation and acquire the skills for meaningful change.

6 Assessment: Observing, Interpreting, and Implementing

"You see the bad situation we are in, that Jerusalem is desolate and its gates burned by fire. Come, let us rebuild the wall of Jerusalem so that we will no longer be a reproach. I told them how the hand of my God had been favorable to me and also about the king's words which he had spoken to me. Then they said, 'Let us arise and build.' So they put their hands to the good work" (Nehemiah 2:17-18).

In 1803, Thomas Jefferson and James Monroe negotiated a deal with France to purchase the Louisiana Territory, the "Louisiana Purchase." Almost immediately, President Jefferson asked Meriwether Lewis to lead an expedition exploring lands west of the Mississippi River. Lewis chose William Clark as his co-leader for the mission and assembled a group later called the Corps of Discovery to accompany them on this adventure.

The cast of those who served with Lewis and Clark were as diverse as any community in America today. "Consider York, William Clark's slave and fellow adventurer, or Pierre Cruzatte, the one-eyed fiddle player, who was part French and part Omaha Indian.

There was German-born Pvt. John Pitts, a miller by trade and a soldier most likely by necessity. Here is Sacagawea, a Shoshone woman who spent formative years with the Hidatsa Indians, and Jean Baptiste Charbonneau, a child of mixed Shoshone-French ancestry. Imagine the sounds around the campfire...This is the crazy quilt that was and is America."[4]

For centuries, nations looked for the waterway that led from the Missouri River to the Pacific Ocean. Finding the route offered tremendous advantages to the nation that discovered it. Lewis and Clark and their Corps of Discovery team were on the verge of accomplishment when they made a discovery they had not anticipated.

"Fifteen months of hard travel, a seemingly endless string of days of backbreaking upstream slogging had led to this moment. Meriwether Lewis recalled all that he had endured: Nervous nights in a strange land. Mosquitoes galore. A dark, cold winter. Grizzly bears. A month-long portage around an immense waterfall. The death of a companion."[5]

"President Thomas Jefferson had indeed commissioned Lewis and Clark and the Corps of Discovery for just this moment, declaring that they should find the cherished water route that everyone believed existed and would ensure the young nation's prosperity: 'the most direct and practicable water communication across this continent, for the purposes of commerce.'"[6]

For nearly three hundred years explorers from Spain, France, England, and America believed that beyond the Missouri River was a waterway that would lead directly to the Pacific Ocean. The nation that controlled that waterway held strategic advantage for the development of this vast region. The common assumption was the land beyond the River was similar to that leading up to the

River. After fighting the battle of moving along upstream, the new channel would take them downstream to their destination. The pioneers who found the highly prized Northwest Passage would fulfill the challenge of the President and become famous for their discovery.

> "After fifteen months of going upstream they looked forward to letting the current swiftly whisk them to the Pacific Ocean. They would crest the hill; find the stream and coast to the finish line.
>
> They could not have been more disappointed.
>
> What Lewis actually discovered was that three hundred years of experts had all been completely and utterly wrong. In front of him was not a gentle slope down to a navigable river running to the Pacific Ocean but the Rocky Mountains. Stretching out for miles and miles as far as the eyes could see was one set of peaks after another."[7]

"At that moment everything that Meriwether Lewis assumed about his journey changed."[8] The band of explorers, the Corps of Discovery, based all of their preparation and equipment on an assumption that proved to be false. They brought the skills and canoes to take them to the conclusion of their search. Now that they faced mountains more extreme than ever imagined, they didn't need better canoes. They needed a whole new paradigm.

Tod Bolsinger's book, *Canoeing the Mountains: Christian Leadership in Uncharted Territory*, is a wakeup call to all who wish to be transformational leaders who plan to approach an uncertain future using the same tools, methods, and techniques that we have relied on in the past. He quotes Bob Johansen, Distinguished Fellow of the Institute for the Future, who states, "After centuries of stability and slow, incremental change, in less than a generation our world has become VUCA: volatile, uncertain, complex, and ambiguous."[9] And this was before the pandemic of 2020.

Churches in America have operated effectively for centuries in an environment that was largely supportive of its worldview. However, globalization, urbanization, and multiculturalism challenge old assumptions. The pandemic, social unrest, and economic uncertainties portray a future much different from the past. Even prior to Covid-19, the West was already facing a decline in church attendance and a growing number of individuals who declared "none" as their religious preference. After months of church closures because of the virus and members attending electronically, if at all, will church life realistically be expected to return to business as usual once a cure for the virus is found?

When Lesslie Newbigin retired to Great Britain after serving as a missionary for forty years in India, he found a more difficult mission field than the one he left behind. He wrote, "England is a pagan society and the development of a truly missionary encounter with this very tough form of paganism is the greatest intellectual and practical task facing the Church."[10] Newbigin made that statement in the 1970's. What was true then is more urgent today.

Astoundingly, 80% of the world lives in areas subject to some form of religious persecution. Millions have fled their homes because of violence and live in refugee camps, or on the streets, or without shelter facing storms, disease, hunger, and exposure. Thousands of children are kidnapped and many sold as sex or domestic slaves. Pastors from Northern Nigeria told our 21Wilberforce team that there were as many as 2,000 girls being held captive by Boko Haram at this time. We have spoken to parents of girls who were kidnapped and who have not been rescued and listened to their heart-rending stories about how they are constantly preoccupied worrying about their daughters and wondering what they may be experiencing. One mother told us she was afraid that she was neglecting her other three children because of constant concern about the daughter who was taken.

The year 2020 may prove to be the wakeup call that churches, universities, businesses, and all walks of life need to realize, to awaken us from our apathy. Better canoes will not help us navigate the Rocky Mountains. Covid-19 knows no geographical boundaries; yet, at the same time, our world confronts a common silent enemy, protection from the crisis has demanded isolation. Schools, businesses, churches, and sporting events were shut down almost overnight. Fear, frustration, and anger spilled over into the streets and throughout social media. Oppressive governments used the pandemic to increase control of individuals' basic human rights. The vulnerable suffered the most.

Our world cries out for transformational leaders like Wilberforce who will stand up to injustice and support goodness. Christopher Wright, the Anglican missiologist said, "It is not so much that God has a mission for his church in the world, but that God has a church for his mission in the world."[11] Into this world of chaos and pain, the church is confronted with an opportunity to be the presence of Christ, feeding the hungry, serving the sick, being advocates for the oppressed.

Leaders are needed both globally and locally who will assess the situation, carefully observe the needs and opportunities, and seek new ways to be God's church in the world.

In the first chapter of Nehemiah we recognize that Nehemiah didn't listen to the words of his brother Hanani about the devastation of Jerusalem and rush away to fix the problem. First he fasted and prayed and sought the word of the Lord. He began to formulate a plan needed for a project to restore Jerusalem and then he had the patience to wait for God to open the door for action. In Nehemiah 2, when God did open the door for him to act and the king asked Nehemiah what troubled him, he was ready with an answer and told Artaxerxes what was on his mind.

When Nehemiah arrived in Jerusalem he immediately assessed the problem. He and a small group of men went out at night and inspected the wall. The walls of the city were in shambles. The once proud city had become a mockery of her previous splendor and a disgrace for God who was worshiped there. Then he called the people together and said to them, "You see the bad situation we are in, that Jerusalem is desolate and its gates burned by fire. Come, let us rebuild the wall of Jerusalem so that we will no longer be a reproach. I told them how the hand of my God had been favorable to me and also about the king's words which he had spoken to me. Then they said, 'Let us arise and build.' So they put their hands to the good work" (Nehemiah 2:17-18).

In 2008, I was invited to become the Executive Director of the Baptist General Convention of Texas. Even though we had been away from Texas for about fifteen years, Texas Baptists were still in many ways my spiritual family. The convention was home to about 5700 churches, eight universities, four children's homes, student ministers on over one hundred college campuses, and numerous other incredible ministries. Unfortunately, 2008 was also the year of the great economic crisis. After I arrived, I began to see the difficult situation facing us including the realization that half of our endowments were wiped out and hundreds of our churches had left or were leaving for a sister Baptist convention. Ignoring the crisis was not an option; we had to make some changes.

Many of my denominational heroes were on the staff of Texas Baptists. As somewhat of an outsider, I knew I couldn't resolve this crisis alone. I brought together a few dozen of the key leaders and we began meeting together to assess the situation. We had so many ministries, and in some ways we were more like a stagnated swamp instead of a flowing river. I was not equipped to decide which ministries were more urgent than others. The entire team of leaders needed to make that assessment. I simply led them through the process. We didn't need to "thin" our organization by taking across the board percentage cuts; we needed to "narrow" it, funding those most strategic to our ministry and eliminating those not as essential. We had lengthy discussions with all of the staff and numerous conversations by departments. I asked the Interim Executive Director to stay on our staff for a few months during the transition and his wisdom and guidance were invaluable.

We had an off-campus meeting where we used the tool Jim Collins recommends in his book *Good to Great,* called the "Hedgehog Concept." "A Hedgehog Concept is a simple, crystalline concept that flows from a deep understanding about the intersection of the following three circles: 1. What can you be the best in the world at? 2. What drives your economic engine? 3. What are you deeply passionate about?"[12]

All of our leaders attempted to answer these questions personally, as a part of a small group and within the larger group. We were not trying to say what we wished we were passionate about or what we desired to do well or what we coveted as our resources. We discussed our heritage, attempted to understand our corporate DNA, assessed our effectiveness ,and attempted to answer the three questions. Each question and the responses were listed inside separate circles and then the three circles overlapped. Where they intersected, we determined our vision.

These discussions led to some of the most difficult decisions I have ever faced in my vocational life. The staff was drastically reduced, including the elimination of whole departments. Leaders of ministries themselves came to us and said our team needs to be phased out. Those few months were painful but by the grace of God, the leadership of some remarkable people on that staff addressed the crisis and clarity was beginning to come.

Those discussions brought us together with a new vision that we called, Hope 2010. As we discussed what we were passionate about it was clear that we all wanted to share the hope of Christ with every person in our state. We were also aware of the marginalized and knew thousands of children failed to have the most basic essential, a nutritious meal. Therefore we adopted a vision statement: *By 2010 we will share the hope of Christ with every person in our state within their own language and context and will make sure that every person has a nutritious meal every day.* Even though we missed our goal it sharpened our focus, changed our narrative, and helped to pull a very diverse group of Baptists of different languages, cultures, and ethnicities toward a common Kingdom assignment.

A leader cannot recommend action until the leader and the team discerns the situation. "Just like a doctor who does not want to prescribe a medicine until she or he has done a proper diagnosis, leaders need to take the time to insure that they have clearly seen the challenge before attempting a new program or making a big change."[13] Tod Bolsinger identifies three phases of the process to assess the situation*: observation, interpretations, and interventions.*[14]

"The first task of a leadership team is to get as many different *observations* that are as objective as possible about the situation."[15]

In the church where Bolsinger was the pastor they interviewed a cross-section of people they had not seen in worship for three months. They asked three questions:

- When were you most excited or felt the sense of deepest connection to our church? What was happening during that time in your life and in the life of our church?
- What has changed in your life or in the life of the church since then that may have affected your sense of connection or excitement about our church?
- What is the one wish/hope/dream you have for the future of our church?[16]

The second part of the process is *interpretation*. What does the data mean? Are there cultural shifts affecting the mission of the church? How have changes in the demographics of the community changed: such as new racial identities, shifts in the ages of the population, new language groups, new technologies, or shifts in cultural attitudes? How will these changes affect the mission and ministry of the church? Are there apparent unmet needs that open doors of outreach for the church, such as ESL classes or afterschool activities?

The response to the survey revealed themes that indicated larger relational dynamics that were unrelated to Sunday morning worship.

- They were more connected when the children were in the youth group.
- They got out of habit of attending church when the husband retired and they began traveling more.
- We used to be really excited before (one of the former associate pastors) left to take another call.[17]

Bolsinger's congregation didn't have a worship service problem but were in the middle of a larger challenge. "Our church was not particularly good at helping people stay connected through life and church transitions."[18] This conclusion brought competing values that led to difficult dilemmas:

- Do we serve our longtime church members who pay the bills, or do we innovate to reach new people and risk angering the stakeholders?
- Do we have a mostly professional staff that provides excellence in ministry program, or do we want a strong, involved laity to use their gifts?
- Do we want a centralized organization unified around clear objectives, or do want a more creative, collaborative system that is nimble, innovative and able to experiment with new ideas?

"Competing values are difficult to navigate because each is valuable."[19]

"Once we have made observations and interpretations, the next step in the adaptive learning process is experimenting with *interventions*. Without question the hardest part of an adaptive learning process is to keep people from jumping to interventions too early."[20] "At the intervention stage there are three principles that must be embraced in order to keep the system calm enough to move forward, make the adaptive shifts necessary and implement new solutions."[21]

- The eventual solution will be a healthy adaptation of the church DNA.
- Interventions should start out modestly and playfully.
- Innovative interventions will always be resisted.

When a pastor arrives to lead a new congregation, or a CEO from outside an organization begins, the first step of observation is essential. Before leading an organization to embrace change, or prior to implementing a strategy that may have worked in another situation, the leader must learn all he or she can about the new church: its history, DNA, heroes, celebrations, non-negotiable values, reputation, and dreams. If the church or organization has a written history, study it. Interview key leaders of the church who are still faithful and even some who may have left. Interview folks in the community. Is the community changing? How do outsiders view the church?

I have asked the pastor selection committee in some churches where I served to remain active for several months as unofficial committees to help me observe a congregation or community. At the same time official key leaders must be engaged in observation. This is especially true when a congregation or institution faces a crisis.

The challenges of 2020 including the pandemic and social unrest have permanently altered society. Churches, universities, health care, government services, and entertainment have all been affected. Some of us may have learned we can exist without network television or professional sports. Will universities continue to rely on sports revenue to expand facilities? Will classroom learning be replaced or supplemented through remote education? Will political conventions or denominational assemblies be replaced by virtual events?

Even though the virus and social unrest have been horrendous, society is presented with an opportunity to confront new realities. Just as Lewis and Clark were forced to shift their strategy when they found mountains instead of a waterway, monumental global interruptions demand new paradigms. In what ways has your ministry or organization been forced to adapt to unexpected challenges?

Endnotes

[1] Todd Bolsinger, *Canoeing the Mountains*, 42.

[2] James M. Kouzes and Barry Z. Posner, *The Leadership Challenge, Fourth Edition*, (San Francisco, CA: John Wiley and Sons, 2007), 14.

[3] Ibid.

[4] James P. Ronda, "Why Lewis and Clark Matter," *Smithsonian Magazine*, August 2003.

[5] Bolsinger, *Canoeing the Mountain*, 24.

[6] Ibid., 25.

[7] Ibid., 26.

[8] Ibid., 27.

[9] Ibid.

[10] Ibid., 29.

[11] Ibid., 30.

[12] Jim Collins, *Good to Great*, (New York, NY: HarperCollins, 2001), 95-96.

[13] Bolsinger, *Canoeing the Mountains*, 111-112.

[14] Ibid., 112.

[15] Ibid.

[16] Ibid., 113-114.

[17] Ibid., 116.

[18] Ibid., 116.

[19] Ibid., 119.

[20] Ibid., 120.

[21] Ibid.

7

Competence: Acquiring Skills for Accomplishing a Task

"Be diligent to present yourself approved to God as a workman who does not need to be ashamed, accurately handling the word of truth" (2 Timothy 2:15).

Competence is a requirement for *emergent leaders* to be able to lead with excellence. Emotion and passion alone will not bring about systemic changes. A person may be given a title but trust and respect must be earned.

On Friday evening, July 26, 1833, just days before William Wilberforce's death on Monday morning, July 29, he received word the goal he had worked for all of his political life was achieved, the House of Commons had just passed the bill abolishing slavery in the British Empire. The overthrow of the horrendous practice of slavery doesn't happen overnight and a single individual does not accomplish it. Much of the groundwork for the abolition of slavery happened decades before the historic action taken by the British House. As God called individuals from various backgrounds to challenge this unjust practice of slavery, these leaders worked diligently to sharpen their skills as they opposed this oppressive evil.

In 1765, Granville Sharp met a young black slave from Barbados, Jonathan Strong, who had been badly beaten by his master. Sharp's advocacy on behalf of this young slave opened Sharp's eyes to the inhumane practice of slavery. His advocacy on behalf of Strong made a name for Sharp as the "protector of the Negro." For several years he studied English law and gained formidable knowledge of the law regarding individual liberty.

After the Zong incident with the massacre of 132 slaves who were thrown overboard, Sharp immediately became involved in the case that finally resulted in the judge's ruling that the owners of the Zong were not entitled to insurance payments for the slaves.

Granville Sharp relied on his incredible intellect and the discipline of research to begin to fight against this evil. In 1769, Granville published his first major tract against slavery, *A Representation of the injustice and dangerous tendency of admitting the least claim of private property in the persons of men, in England.* He sought to change the minds of British judges and lawyers who believed it was legal to bring and keep slaves in England.

Although Sharp had little formal educational training, he was a lifelong learner. He was a gifted musician; some said he had the best bass voice in all of England. In addition, he played numerous musical instruments including the clarinet, oboe, flageolet, kettledrums, harp, and a double-flute that he made himself. He often signed his notes G#.

Sharp was a faithful member of the Church of England and visited many bishops in person as well as writing the Archbishop of Canterbury urging them to stand united for the abolition of slavery. He became a credible theologian and when he was criticized for having no theological training, he taught himself Greek and Hebrew and became a classical grammarian. The Granville Sharp Rule was named for him because of a study he presented in defense of the deity of Christ. He published nearly seventy books and pamphlets addressing topics from abolition to the pronunciation of biblical Hebrew, to agriculture, and music. Three of his publications were in French and the rest in English.

Granville's credibility as an intellect, skilled writer, and dedicated advocate began to reshape the hearts and minds of his generation about slavery. He and other gifted men and women of great skills and tenacity never gave up in their fight against slavery prior to its ultimate abolition in England.

The movement that led to the overthrow of the racist policies of segregation in the U.S. in the 1960's, was spearheaded by Martin Luther King, Jr. His father, Martin Luther King, Sr. was one of the primary influences on his son. MLK, Jr. speaks of his dad's commanding presence; he was over 220 pounds. Martin's father's confidence and his courage inspired him; but most of all he was influenced by his father's consistent Christian character.

Martin Luther King, Jr. encountered the discrimination of segregation early in his life and often. When he was only six years of age a treasured friendship was forbidden because of race; the young white friend was told that he could no longer play with Martin because Martin was Black, and he was White. When Martin brought this up at dinner his parents began to explain the tragedies of racism. At this early age, he began to hate every white person. He said, "How could I love a race of people who hated me and who had been responsible for breaking me up with one of my best childhood friends?"[1]

This resentment was reinforced often by separate schools, separate swimming pools, being moved to chairs in the back of a store when purchasing shoes, being slapped by a white woman and called the "n" word who accused him of stepping on her foot, forced to give up a seat on the bus when white passengers entered, and other acts of dehumanizing Blacks.

"The first time I was seated behind a curtain in a dining car, I felt as if the curtain had been dropped on my selfhood. I could never adjust to the separate waiting rooms, separate eating places, separate rest rooms, partly because the separate was always unequal, and partly because the very idea of separation did something to my sense of dignity and self-respect."[2]

King was faced with the same choices that confront all of us when we are exposed to injustice: do we just accept it as just the way things are, do we resent the situation and live a life of bitterness, or do we become determined to work for justice. "And what does the Lord require of you but to do justice, to love kindness, and to walk humbly with your God?" (Micah 6:8). MLK chose to work for justice.

King said, "My call to the ministry was not a miraculous or supernatural something. On the contrary it was an inner urge calling me to serve humanity."[3] "I became convinced that noncooperation with evil is as much a moral obligation as is cooperation with good."[4] Martin knew this calling required his very best. "I revolted, too, against the emotionalism of much Negro religion, the shouting and stamping, I didn't understand it, and it embarrassed me. I often say if we, as a people, had as much religion in our hearts and souls as we have in our legs and feet, we could change the world."[5]

King committed himself to acquire the knowledge and competence required to challenge the injustice of segregation. He received his Bachelor of Arts degree in sociology from Morehouse College in Atlanta on June 8, 1948, and his Bachelor of Divinity degree from Crozer Seminary in Upland, Pennsylvania, on May 8, 1951.

While at Crozer Seminary, he began a serious intellectual quest for a method to eliminate social evil, studying philosophers Plato, Aristotle, Rousseau, Hobbes, Bentham, Mill, and Locke. King believed that preaching was one of the most vital needs of our society, if used correctly. His study of Rauschenbusch convinced him, "that any religion that professes concern for the souls of men and is not equally concerned about the slums that damn them, the economic conditions that strangle them, and the social conditions that cripple them is a spiritually moribund religion only waiting for the day to be buried."[6]

King carefully scrutinized the writings of Marx and Lenin including Marx' *Das Kapital,* and *The Communist Manifesto,* written by Marx and Friedrich Engels. He concluded, "First, I rejected their materialistic interpretation of history. Second, I strongly disagreed with communism's ethic relativism...consequently almost anything—force, violence, murder, lying—is a justifiable means to the 'millennial' end. Third, I opposed communism's political totalitarianism. This deprecation of individual freedom was objectionable to me. I am convinced now, as I was then, that man is an end because he is a child of God."[7] However, Marx did reveal "the danger of the profit motive as the sole basis of an economic system: capitalism is always in danger of inspiring men to be more concerned about making a living than making a life."[8]

The life and teachings of Mahatma Gandhi were probably most influential in King's development of nonviolent resistance. "As I delved deeper into the philosophy of Gandhi, my skepticism concerning the power of love gradually diminished, and I came to see for the first time its potency in the area of social reform."[9] "Gandhi was probably the first person in history to lift the love ethic of Jesus above mere interaction between individuals to a powerful and effective social force on a large scale. It was in this Gandhian emphasis on love and nonviolence that I discovered the method for social reform that I had been seeking."[10]

King's quest for competence in ministry continued throughout his life. He earned a doctorate in systematic theology from Boston University on June 5, 1955. The Sermon on the Mount in Matthew 5—7 was influential on the development of his theology and philosophy of life just as it was with Gandhi. In one of King's early messages he concluded, "I'm not going to put my ultimate faith in the little gods that can be destroyed in an atomic age, but the God who has been our help in ages past, and our hope for years to come, and our shelter in the time of storm, and our eternal home. That's the God that I'm putting my ultimate faith in...The God that I'm talking about this morning is the God of the universe and the God that will last through the ages. If we are to go forward this morning, we've got to go back and find that God. That is the God that demands and commands our ultimate allegiance."[11]

Martin Luther King, Jr. and Granville Sharp are two examples of why competence is a requirement for transformational leaders. Change requires the best of us. Standing against injustice is a lifelong commitment of individuals and teams creating movements that confront evil and stand up for the oppressed. Parents, pastors, professors, politicians, and all in positions of influence over their children, their congregations, their students, and their constituents must offer their very best in sharpening the tools and gifts God has given them to fulfill their Kingdom assignment.

Endnotes

[1] Carson, *The Autobiography of Martin Luther King, Jr.*, 7.

[2] Ibid., 12.

[3] Ibid., 13.

[4] Ibid., 14.

[5] Ibid., 15.

[6] Ibid., 18.

[7] Ibid., 20.

[8] Ibid., 21.

[9] Ibid., 23.

[10] Ibid., 24.

[11] Ibid., 33.

8

Character: Clarifying and Prioritizing Your Values

"The things which you heard from me in the presence of many witnesses, entrust these to faithful men who will be able to teach others also" (2 Timothy 2:2).

Leaders model the way. "Titles are granted, but it's your behavior that wins you respect. As Tom Brack, with Europe's Smart-Team AG, told us, 'Leading means you have to be a good example, and live what you say.'"[1]

Emergent leaders must lead by example. In 2 Timothy 2:2, the Apostle Paul instructs Timothy to keep four generations in mind when making disciples. Paul represents the first generation; Timothy represents the second, then Timothy was to train those who will train others.

In his letter to the Philippians, Paul writes, "The things you have learned and received and heard and seen in me, practice these things, and the God of peace will be with you" (Philippians 4:9).

On the surface, Paul's statements appear arrogant. However his life affirmed these commands. Basically, Paul told Timothy and the church in Philippi to "come follow me follow Jesus." That statement certainly has more credibility than one who says, "Do as I say not as I do." Paul lived in such a way that he encouraged others to scrutinize his behavior and see if his actions affirmed his values. Paul was one who "Modeled the Way."

Tillie Burgin is one of my heroes. She and her family served as missionaries in South Korea for a decade but had to return to her hometown Arlington, Texas, because of a family medical issue. Even though she had a wonderful position with the Arlington School District she continued to pray about her next Kingdom assignment. She asked herself if we can do missions in Korea, why can we not do missions in Arlington? Tillie recalled to me in a personal conversation of harassing her pastor about a ministry position with the church, until finally, like the persistent widow in Luke 18, the pastor offered her a part-time job.

During her first week on the job, a woman in need of financial assistance was sent to Tillie. Tillie helped her with her request and then invited her to church the next Sunday. Amazingly, the woman did meet her at church but it was obviously a very awkward moment for both of them. In spite of the hospitality of the church, the guest certainly was out of place. Tillie went to the woman's modest apartment and offered to have a Bible study in her home the next Sunday. Even though she must have been reluctant she agreed to host them and said she would invite some of her friends to join.

That was the beginning of an unbelievable journey. On August 1, 1986, Mission Arlington was started. In the Mission Arlington website under Core Values we read,

> "When Mission Arlington began the idea was to help people find their way back into church. We subsequently discovered that many people felt disconnected from the church in general. It's not that churches weren't friendly or inviting, but that there seemed to be some barrier in the minds and hearts of people, making it difficult to connect. We decided then that if people couldn't come to the church, for whatever reason, we would take the church to them.
>
> Today people of all ages gather each week to hear the Bible taught in multiple languages in 349 locations in Arlington and the larger Dallas/Fort Worth region. We meet in neighborhood homes, apartment club houses, mobile home parks and in any other location where people can gather together to hear God's Word."[2]

Mission Arlington (also named Mission Metroplex) understands there is a connection between the physical and the spiritual and wants to meet the physical needs of people whenever possible. They have a conviction that every life is important to God and therefore important to them. As a result, they attempt to meet the needs of every person who comes through their doors.

Mission Arlington may have never happened without the strong support and faithful prayers of First Baptist Church of Arlington. As the ministry grew, hundreds of volunteers, including youth and adults, offer almost every conceivable resource for folks in need. These include:

- Health Care (dental, medical, counseling, medical equipment, support groups)
- Bible Studies and Church Congregations

- Children and Youth (After school, school supplies, summer services)
- Holiday Events (The Christmas Store provided gifts to 32,691 children in 2019)
- Groceries
- Furniture
- Transportation

If a person asks Tillie Burgin who is responsible for this amazing story she will quickly give all the credit to the Lord. And of course she is correct. However, if we ask anyone connected with Mission Arlington who is the one God has used to inspire, encourage, lead, and direct the ministry all will say Tillie Burgin. Even though Tillie reached retirement age several years ago, she has not retired and continues to work as hard and is committed as any other staff member or volunteers. Mission Arlington reflects her values of a passion for Christ, a love for all people, a drive for excellence in all things, and a determined work ethic.

Over seventy-five thousand people from around the globe have responded to a survey from Kouzes and Posner called "Characteristics of Admired Leaders." The responses didn't vary significantly even when considering demographical, organizational, or cultural differences. Over time only four values, out of a list of twenty, consistently received over 60 percent of the votes: honesty, forward-looking, inspirational, competent.[3] "In almost every survey we've conducted, honesty has been selected more often than any other leadership characteristic; overall, it emerges as the single most important factor in the leader-constituent relationship. It is clear that if people anywhere are to willingly follow someone—whether it's into battle or into the boardroom, the front office or the front lines—they first want to assure themselves that the person is worthy of their trust."[4]

Credibility is the foundation of leadership. "Here are some common phrases people use to describe how they know credibility when they see it:

- They practice what they preach.
- They walk the talk.
- Their actions are consistent with their words.
- They put their money where their mouth is.
- They follow through on their promises.
- They do what they say they will do."[5]

The Kouzes-Posner First Law of Leadership: "If you don't believe in the messenger, you won't believe the message."[6] The Kouzes-Posner Second Law of Leadership: "Do what you say you will do."[7]

Emergent leaders must clarify their values and work to insure that their organization knows and shares those common values. How do you know what you value? Some questions you may ask yourself to clarify your values:

- What keeps you awake at night?
- What are your non-negotiable beliefs?
- What brings you sorrow or offers you joy?
- What are you passionate about?

In the *Leadership Challenge Workbook*, they list over fifty sample values and ask the reader to select five of the values that are most important to them and to their project. A few of the values they include are: Success, Beauty, Courage, Dependability, Diversity, Effectiveness, Family, Freedom, Happiness, Hope, Intelligence, Loyalty, Patience, Quality, Recognition, Respect, Risk-taking, Faith, Teamwork, Trust, Wisdom, Honesty, and Competence.[8]

"Begin the process of clarifying your values by reflecting on your ideal image of yourself—how you would like to be seen by others."[9]

When Jim Collins and his researchers were attempting to learn what caused good companies to become great companies, they were first surprised by how few companies made that leap and then didn't expect leadership to be the common ingredient in the companies that became great. They actually weren't looking for that answer but the conclusion came from empirical evidence. The great companies had leaders that exhibited similar traits. Collins called them Level 5 leaders according to a hierarchy of leaders.

- **Level 5 Executive**: Builds enduring greatness through paradoxical blend of personal humility and professional will.
- **Level 4 Effective Leader**: Catalyzes commitment to and vigorous pursuit of a clear and compelling vision, stimulating higher performance standards.
- **Level 3 Competent Manager**: Organizes people and resources toward the effective and efficient pursuit of predetermined objectives.
- **Level 2 Contributing Team Member**: Contributes individual capabilities to the achievement of group objectives and works effectively with others in a group setting.
- **Level 1 Highly Capable Individual**: Makes productive contributions through talent, knowledge, skills, and good work habits.[10]

As we look at these definitions, we understand that all of these qualities are needed. Not every person is a Level 5 leader, but the Level 5 leader embodies all of these traits. However, I believe the qualities Collins mentions for Level 5 leaders are exactly the traits needed in transformational leaders. Reframing Collins characteristics of Level 5 leaders, I call them emergent leaders.

- *Emergent leaders look out the window to attribute success to factors other than themselves.* When things go poorly, however, they look in the mirror and blame themselves, taking full responsibility. Celebrity leaders do just the opposite—they look in the mirror to take credit for success, but out the window to assign blame for disappointing results.[11]
- *Emergent leaders set up their successors for even greater success in the next generation*, while egocentric leaders often set up their successors for failure.[12]
- *Emergent leaders display a compelling modesty*, are self-effacing and understated.[13]
- *Emergent leaders never want to become larger than life heroes.* They never aspire to be put on a pedestal or become unreachable icons. They seem to be ordinary people quietly producing extraordinary results.[14]
- *Emergent leaders channel their ego needs away from themselves and into the larger goal of building a great company.* It's not that these leaders have no ego or self-interest, they are incredibly ambitious—but ambition is first and foremost for the institution, not themselves.[15]

The Apostle Paul and Tillie Burgin lead by example. They modeled the way. High impact leaders are player-coaches or working-foremen that prioritize their values by practicing what they preach.

Endnotes

[1] Kouzes and Posner, 15.

[2] Quote and statistics about Mission Arlington comes from Mission Arlington website: www.missionarlington.org.

[3] Kouzes and Posner, *The Leadership Challenge*, 29.

[4] Ibid., 32.

[5] Ibid., 40.

[6] Ibid., 47.

[7] Ibid., 41.

[8] Ibid., 35-36.

[9] Ibid., 69.

[10] Collins, *Good to Great*, 20.

[11] Ibid., 39. [I have substituted the word "emergent" where Collins used the words Level 5 Leader].

[12] Ibid., 26.

[13] Ibid., 27.

[14] Ibid., 28.

[15] Ibid., 21.

9

Vision: Inspiring a Shared Vision

"But you will receive power when the Holy Spirit has come upon you; and you shall be My witnesses both in Jerusalem, and in all of Judea and Samaria, and even to the remotest part of the earth" (Acts 1:8).

Leaders inspire a shared vision. "When people described to us their personal-best leadership experiences, they told of times when they imagined an exciting, highly attractive future for their organization. They had visions and dreams of what could be. They had absolute and total personal belief in those dreams, and they were confident in their abilities to make extraordinary things happen. Every organization and every social movement, begins with a dream. The dream or vision is the force that invents the future."[1]

Jesus' vision for His followers was clear, compelling, and bold. By God's grace, they were able to accomplish this mission because Jesus prepared them and the Holy Spirit empowered them.

Nehemiah had a vision of a city fortified by a rebuilt wall. The Apostle Paul desired to take the gospel all the way to Spain. Wilberforce saw the evil practice of slavery abolished. Martin Luther

King, Jr. had a dream of a world where people would not be judged by the color of their skin. Tillie Burgin saw the church going to the people rather than people coming to a church.

Each of these transformational leaders had a very clear picture in their mind of a destination conceived, but not yet realized, which would require a movement of like-minded individuals empowered by God and willing to pay the price to see it happen.

"The human being is the only animal that thinks about the future,"[2] writes Daniel Gilbert, professor of psychology at Harvard University. "The greatest achievement of the human brain is its ability to imagine objects and episodes that do not exist in the realm of the real, and it is this ability that allows us to think about the future…the human brain is an anticipation machine, and making future is the most important thing it does."[3] "You begin with the end in mind, by knowing what you dream about accomplishing, and then figure out how to make it happen."[4]

Dr. Hormoz Shariat, Founder and President of IranAlive, has a dream to reach one million Muslims for Christ in his homeland of Iran. This vision was completely different from his earlier goal of getting a Ph.D from an American university and making a lot of money. Hormoz, like William Wilberforce, needed a spiritual awakening before he would clearly understand his ultimate life ambition. Also like Wilberforce his great change came after a period of deep reflection and personal agony. In his book, *Iran's Great Awakening,* Shariat wrote,

> "The drive down the San Gabriel Mountains provides a beautiful view of Los Angeles. It was January 1979, and I was full of excitement and great optimism for my future. Iran was on its way to becoming a democracy, and I was well on my way to achieving my dreams. But something was

> missing in my life. Life in the United States was comfortable, but I was not satisfied. Like many others who came to America, I expected to live happily ever after. I didn't expect to feel so miserable inside. I was achieving my dreams, so why wasn't I happy? Why did I feel empty inside? Why did life feel meaningless? I thought that if I got a degree and found a good job, I would be happy. To me, there were only two kinds of people: those who achieved their life goals and those who did not. If I were falling short of my goals, then I would have reason to feel frustrated. But I was achieving my dreams, yet still felt empty and depressed."[5]

Hormoz was born in Iran into a Muslim family. He met his wife Donnell when they were both in college. She was an American girl from Oregon who moved to Tehran to work for DuPont, a global science company. She was a nominal Christian but converted to Islam when they decided to get married. "She was touched by the devotion of Muslims. She admired their focus on the faith and their families. When she compared Islam to the lukewarm Christianity she saw in her church, she was drawn to Islam. We were married in Tehran on October 23, 1977."[6] This was just a couple of years prior to the Iranian Revolution and the overthrow of the Shah.

"The Shah had become so unpopular that even the students and other intellectuals became militant. Donnell was so shaken by two violent attacks she experienced that she donned the chador (an Islamic cloak) and joined me on Tehran's streets shouting, 'Death to Shah! Death to America!'"[7]

Hormoz even joined with Donnell and the mobs in their protest saying, "Death to America!" "However, while my lips were proclaiming death to the United States, in my heart I was pleading, 'But not yet. I want to get my PhD from a good American university!'"[8]

A few years later, Shariat's dreams were coming true. He believed Iran was moving toward democracy and he was in America pursuing his academic goals. Yet Hormoz felt empty and his marriage was headed for divorce.

> "I decided to study the Quran one more time—but as a researcher this time. I would be objective and study with an open and bias-free mind. I knew my intelligence and sincere heart would not lead me astray.
>
> If there was truth in the Quran, I should be able to find it. I purchased a Quran (in Farsi and Arabic) and started studying it with a new zeal and hunger for the truth. I decided that if I found God in the Quran, then I would dedicate the rest of my life to serving Allah and telling others about Islam. It took me only three months to complete an intense study of the Quran. I already knew most of the material I encountered, but I did learn a few new things. But my heart was still empty. I was not changed. What's more, I still hadn't encountered the God I searched for so diligently."[9]

A janitor where Donnell worked began telling her about Jesus and led her to Christ. Hormoz believed that as a scientist he must be open-minded in his search for truth and decided to read the Bible.

> "I had planned to read the whole Bible in about three days, but three months later I was still early in Matthew's Gospel (chapter 5) and struggling with everything Jesus said. One night I got so angry that I threw my Bible under the bed."[10]

Later Hormoz recovered the Bible and continued to read until he gave his heart to the Lord. The brilliant scientist didn't find Jesus in the complexities of life but in the simplicity of His message. Hormoz recalls his journey,

> "What's more, knowing God, experiencing His presence, and being changed by His transforming power were not complicated. You did not need to be an intellectual with an advanced degree to understand it. Even a child can understand it. That simple message changed my wife and me. It saved our marriage. Sometimes, when I challenge people for evangelism, I say, 'The janitor at Donnell's company, who didn't speak English, led her to Christ. So, what's your excuse for not sharing the Gospel?'"[11]

Coming to Christ did not end the struggles for Hormoz and Donnell but by the grace of God their marriage was healed and God has given them an incredible ministry together. After his conversion, Hormoz continued his education and was hired for his dream job. As a new believer, he shared his faith publicly even on the streets of California and helped start churches for Iranian believers. He was led to leave his job and rely completely on his life as a pastor, which brought its own frustrations and challenges. Many of his sincere efforts ended in failure and criticism from his fellow Christians.

When he was just a few months old in the Lord, he learned that the Islamic government had arrested his brother Hamraz on some minor political charges. For two years the government continued to tell Hormoz' mother that her son was fine and was saying his prayers while in prison. Then suddenly one day she received a call to retrieve her son's body. He had been executed. They wouldn't release his body to her until she paid them for the cost of the firing-squad bullets that ended her son's life.

Hormoz couldn't help but have anger at those who killed his brother. How could he ever share the gospel with them? But God led him to read 1 Peter 2:9, "But you are A CHOSEN RACE, A ROYAL PRIESTHOOD, A HOLY NATION, A PEOPLE FOR GOD'S OWN POSSESSION, so that you may proclaim the excellences of Him who has called you out of darkness into His marvelous light."

> "This verse encouraged me so much. I recommitted my life to the Lord—I would never stop evangelizing and loving others. I dedicated my life to sharing the Gospel. I prayed that **God would use me to help one million Muslims to come to Christ** during my lifetime. But at the time, I had no idea how this goal could ever be accomplished."[12]

You will have to read Hormoz Shariat's book, *Iran's Great Awakening,* to see how God has directed them to establish a television network that now shares the hope of Christ with millions of Iranians every day, twenty-four hours a day.

"In January 2012, we started Iran Alive's Network 7 Channel, broadcasting around the clock in the Middle East, North Africa, and Europe."[13]

> "One thing we know: We cannot do it alone. God is using other ministries also to accomplish His purposes in Iran. We simply focus on doing our part faithfully and with excellence. We ask God for gifted preachers and teachers to join us. And we pray for Christian businessmen, government officials, media leaders, and gifted artists to join us in our efforts. We pray for partners of all kinds to join us to impact Iran, and to reach one million Muslims for Christ."[14]

In September of 2020, I asked Dr. Shariat how the Covid-19 pandemic affected their ministry. Hormoz said, "It has increased conversions ten-fold. Prior to the virus we had fifty people contacting us from Iran every week sharing about their new faith in Christ, but since then we have been hearing from an average of five hundred each week." The prayer of Hormoz to reach a million Iranians for Christ no longer appears to be an impossible vision.

When Jesus commissioned His few followers to make disciples of all the nations according to Matthew 28:18-20, just prior to His ascension, they may have been overwhelmed with His challenge. The friends of William Wilberforce may have believed he was a dreamer when he challenged Britain to abolish slavery in the 19th century. Some may have heard Martin Luther King, Jr's speech in front of the Lincoln Memorial and thought to themselves that we have heard this challenge before but nothing will change. However, the disciples *did* take the gospel to the nations; the abolition of slavery *did* come to England; and segregation in the South *ended.* When God inspires and empowers a movement, and when men and women say, "Yes," to His calling, justice will ultimately prevail.

Few of us are called to be global leaders like Wilberforce or King. For most of us, we need to understand how to turn-around a declining church, or how to raise teenagers, or how to teach vulnerable children during a pandemic when they are at risk to attend school yet don't have computers to work from home. However, we are reminded that King did not bring about social change alone. It took a movement. Only after Black individuals integrated a white only lunch counter, or sat in a front seat of a bus, or marched to Selma into the face of brutality, were systemic changes secured.

Emergent leaders must know how to inspire a shared vision.

> "Leaders gaze across the horizon of time, imagining the attractive opportunities that are in store when they and their constituents arrive at a distant destination. *They envision exciting and ennobling possibilities.* Leaders have a desire to make something happen, to change the way things are, to create something that no one else has ever created before. In some ways, leaders live their lives backward. They see pictures in their mind's eye of what the results will look like even before they've started their project, much as an architect draws a blueprint or an engineer builds a model. Their clear image of the future pulls them forward. Yet visions seen only by leaders are insufficient to create an organized movement or a significant change in a company. A person with no constituents is not a leader, and people will not follow until they accept a vision as their own. Leaders cannot command commitment, only inspire it."[15]

Setting a clear vision is one of the most critical steps for movements, institutions, companies, and churches in attempting to fulfill their Kingdom assignment. Jim Collins describes the *Hedgehog Concept* is his book, *Good to Great,* which describes three diagnostic questions that are essential for the development of a clear vision. I have used this simple tool as a new pastor of a church, leader of a new seminary, and leader of a denominational organization. The Hedgehog Concept demands leaders look critically at their organization's passions, proficiencies, and resources in order to reach their greatest potential. I have restated the three questions:

- What stirs your greatest passion?
- When are you at your best?
- What are your resources?

"A Hedgehog Concept is not a goal to be the best, a strategy to be the best, an intention to be the best, a plan to be the best. It is an understanding of what you can be the best at. The distinction is absolutely crucial."[16]

"Visionary leaders took a complex world and simplified it."[17] "In a world overrun by management faddists, brilliant visionaries, ranting futurists, fear mongers, motivational gurus, and all the rest, it's refreshing to see a company succeed so brilliantly by taking one simple concept and just doing it with excellence and imagination."[18]

"The Hedgehog Concept requires a severe standard of excellence. It's not just about building on strength and competence, but about understanding what your organization truly has the potential to be the very best at and sticking to it."[19]

A retreat setting is one of the best formats for working through the Hedgehog Concept. Bring key leaders together and challenge them to work individually, in small teams, and with the larger group to answer the three questions. We cannot manufacture passion or "motivate" people to feel passionate. We can only discover what ignites our passion and the passions of those around us. Knowing what we do best forces us to study the history of our organization. When our congregation was at its institutional best, what were the practices that made it effective? What is the DNA of our organization? How would others define what our church does best?

Discerning the resources of an organization is not creating a wish list but a clear recognition of its assets and liabilities. Complacent organizations never ask the right questions. They set their goals and strategies more from bravado than from understanding. A vision is more than just a mindless pursuit of growth.

On April 3, 1968, Martin Luther King, Jr. delivered a speech in support of the striking sanitation workers at Mason Temple in Memphis, Tennessee, the day before he was assassinated. He said,

> "We've got some difficult days ahead. But it doesn't matter with me now. Because I've been to the mountaintop. And I don't mind. Like anybody, I would like to live a long life. Longevity has its place. But I'm not concerned about that now. I just want to do God's will. And He's allowed me to go up to the mountain. And I've looked over. And I've seen the promised land. I may not get there with you. But I want you to know tonight, that we, as a people, will get to the promised land...Mine eyes have seen the glory of the coming of the Lord."[20]

A transformational leader casts a clear vision that often continues to live on generations after his death. Do you have a vision, a calling, for which you are willing to die?

Endnotes

1 Kouzes and Posner, *The Leadership Challenge*, 16-17.

2 Ibid., 106.

3 Ibid.

4 Ibid., 103, quote from Jim Pitts, Northrop Grumman Corporation.

5 Hormoz Shariat, *Iran's Great Awakening*, (Melissa, TX: Iran Alive Ministries, 2020), 4-5.

6 Ibid., 5.

7 Ibid., 7.

8 Ibid.

9 Ibid., 13.

10 Ibid., 14.

11 Ibid., 17.

12 Ibid., 25-26.

13 Ibid., 56.

[14] Ibid., 57.

[15] Collins, *Good to Great*, 17.

[16] Ibid., 98.

[17] Ibid., 91.

[18] Ibid., 93.

[19] Ibid., 100.

[20] Quote from Martin Luther King, Jr. in his speech in Memphis, Tennessee on April 3, 1968, at the Mason Temple.

10

Challenge the Process: Keeping the Memories While Leaving the Memorabilia Behind

"When people think about their personal bests they automatically think about some kind of challenge. Why? The fact is that when times are stable and secure, people are not severely tested. They may perform well, get promoted, even achieve fame and fortune. But certainty and routine breed complacency. In contrast, personal and business hardships have a way of making people come face to face with whom they really are and what they're capable of becoming.

Thus the study of leadership is the study of how men and women guide others through adversity, uncertainty, hardship, disruption, transformation, transition, recovery, new beginnings, and other significant challenges."[1]

Leaders challenge the process.

As previously mentioned in Tod Bolsinger's book, *Canoeing the Mountain*, he described the shock that Lewis and Clark confronted when they realized their preparation for travel to the Pacific Ocean was based on incorrect data, they had to come up with a new paradigm. For hundreds of years the common belief among the Spanish, French, and American explorers was the existence of a waterway that would carry them downstream from the Missouri River to the Pacific. However, instead of a river they found the Rocky Mountains. The canoes they brought with them were of no value for navigating the Rockies.[2]

The year 2020 has been a time of unpredictable catastrophes with the pandemic, social unrest in nations around the world, economic collapse, natural disasters with hurricanes, fires, droughts, flooding, and mass migration of refugees fleeing wars and persecution. After 9/11, life in the United States never returned to normal. Security, travel, and the economy experienced significant changes. The pandemic of 2020 will probably result in even more shifts. Unless churches, universities, businesses, and even entertainment recognize new global realities they may not survive.

Work, education, and worship began to take place remotely. Will worshipers who were allowed to pick their preacher each Sunday, who sat before computer screens in their pajamas sipping coffee, and Bible study groups that were connected by Zoom return to buildings to participate in church activities? Will workers who worked remotely from home return to the grind of a one-hour commute to work to perform many of the tasks they accomplished from their own home offices?

Not many years ago television basically consisted of three or four major networks that gradually increased to additional cable channels. Now they face competition from Netflix, Hulu, Apple TV,

Amazon Prime Video, and Disney +. Even with all of the choices people still complain about finding nothing to watch. A few decades ago, folks received their news from a local daily newspaper that was delivered to their house and listened to Chet Huntley on NBC every evening. Today many local newspapers are closing down and news is available twenty-four hours a day on television, radio, and social media. Some of the magazines that have survived have transitioned from weekly to monthly or even quarterly.

Will students continue to spend hundreds of thousands of dollars to attend universities where they accumulate burdensome debts only to receive degrees that offer no clear path to jobs when they graduate, or will they choose vocational training or online education? Do seminaries expect potential seminarians to leave their homes and jobs to receive residential training for three years only to return to churches that have shifted drastically during the time they were away?

My father's experience as a pastor was far different from mine. He belonged to a denomination that provided all of the resources and training he needed for ministry. All of the churches he served, used the same translation of the Bible, the same hymnal, the same Sunday School curriculum, and the pastors from his denomination all attended denominationally owned and operated seminaries. Funding missions was easy. Each church wrote one check that was distributed for missions, humanitarian assistance, education (both university and graduate), and other ministries deemed necessary for fulfilling the great commission.

Most of the churches had Sunday School and worship the same time each Sunday morning with a format as predictable as liturgical churches. Even church buildings were similar with educational and worship space adequate for accommodating Christmas and Easter services, yet on most Sundays were less than crowded.

My generation has been much more creative. Some have been creative enough to begin an occasional Saturday night service and broadened the music in the worship services adding praise teams, contemporary music, and stage lights. Pastors come from many different seminary experiences and some are so impatient they just skip seminary and learn by doing, a practice I pray the medical profession doesn't adopt.

Some things haven't changed considerably, however. Church is primarily focused on a place and a time (Sunday morning). Church success is typically judged by attendance, baptisms, and budgets. A high priority is placed on buildings, even though some are used for only a few hours a week. Professional paid staff is expected to carry out much of the church functions including leading worship and organizing church activities. The Sunday morning hour continues to be one of the most segregated hours in any community.

Churches in America and Western Europe may be facing a post-pandemic, post-denominational, and even post-Christendom era. Will business as usual enable the church to communicate the power of the gospel to our communities?

The challenges of 2020 have been horrible and brought tremendous grief and suffering to much of our world. However, it also offers an opportunity for churches, institutions, and even businesses to stop and evaluate our priorities and practices.

> *"Leadership isn't so much skillfully helping a group accomplish what they want to do (that is management).* Leadership is taking people where they need to go and yet resist going. Leadership, as I have defined it, is energizing a community of people toward their own transformation in order

to accomplish a shared mission in the face of a changing world. It's about challenging, encouraging and equipping people to be transformed more and more into the kind of community that God can use to accomplish his plans in a particular locale."[3]

"Leadership isn't about challenge for challenge's sake. It's not about shaking things up just to keep people on their toes. It's about challenge for meaning's sake. It's about challenge with passion. It's about living life purposefully. What gets leaders—and all of us, really—through the tough times, the scary times, the times when you don't think you can even get up in the morning or take another step, is a *sense of meaning and purpose.*"[4]

Emergent leaders believe in an atmosphere of risk taking. However, change must occur by taking small steps, generating small wins. During the Civil Rights movement of the 60s and 70s, King and the other leaders found simple, yet profound and challenging steps to take in order to overturn a culture of discrimination. They integrated segregated lunch counters in drug stores, sat in the front of buses where only whites were allowed, led boycotts of public transportation, held marches and rallies, and encouraged voter registration. Each of these acts of resistance led to fierce opposition, yet King and the others never lost faith in the end result, and persevered gaining momentum a step at a time.

"Yes leadership is about vision. But leadership is equally about creating a climate where the truth is heard and the brutal facts confronted. There's a huge difference between the opportunity to 'have your say' and the opportunity to be *heard*. The good-to-great leaders understood the distinction, creating a culture wherein people had a tremendous opportunity to be heard and, ultimately, for the truth to be heard."[5]

Jim Collins offers four basic questions where truth can be heard:

1. Lead with questions, not answers.
2. Engage in dialogue and debate, not coercion.
3. Conduct autopsies, without blame.
4. Build "red flag" mechanisms.[6]

Leaders are not responsible for coming up with the answers and then motivating others to adopt. "It means having the humility to grasp the fact that you do not yet understand enough to have the solutions and then to ask the questions that will lead to the best possible insights."[7]

Life is unpredictable. No one was able to predict the pandemic of 2020. Almost without warning global economies were shut down, buildings were emptied, cities were vacated, events were canceled. Other life interruptions can be just as abrupt and cruel: unexpected illness, grief in the death of someone close to you, loss of job, rejection by a friend or even a family member. Life seems cruel and unpredictable. "You must never confuse faith that you will prevail in the end—which you can never afford to lose—with the discipline to confront the most brutal facts of your current reality, whatever they may be."[8]

Martin Luther King, Jr. knew he may not make it to the Promised Land but he had been to the mountain and saw victory for his people. Moses didn't make it to the Promised Land but he never lost sight of the fact that the Hebrew people would make it. William Wilberforce could have given up on the fight against slavery decade after decade, but he never stopped believing this was the task given to him by God. The Apostle Paul was beaten, whipped, chained, almost killed by stoning, put in prison on many occasions, yet he continued to be full of joy because God had set him free. He wrote to the Romans who themselves were facing persecution and said, "For if we live, we live for the Lord, or if we die, we die for the Lord; therefore whether we live or die, we are the Lord's" (Romans 14:8).

Leaders must challenge their followers to take an honest look at their organizations and ask tough questions about effectiveness. They must also remember that no great work is accomplished alone. In the next chapter, we will discuss the importance of creating a team.

Endnotes

[1] Kouzes and Posner, *The Leadership Challenge*, 164.

[2] Bolsinger, *Canoeing the Mountains*, Ideas conveyed by the author on page 26.

[3] Bolsinger, *Canoeing the Mountains*, 124.

[4] Kouzes and Posner, *The Leadership Challenge*, 173 (Italics added).

[5] Collins, *Good to Great,* 74.

[6] Ibid., 74-78.

[7] Ibid., 75.

[8] Ibid., 85.

11

Creating the Team: Getting the Right People on the Bus

"Moses father-in-law said to him, 'The thing that you are doing is not good. You will surely wear out, both yourself and these people who are with you, for the task is too heavy for you; you cannot do it alone'" (Exodus 18:17-18).

"Grand dreams don't become significant realities through the actions of a single person. It requires a team effort. It requires solid trust and strong relationships. It requires deep competence and cool confidence. It requires group collaboration and individual accountability. To get extraordinary things done in organizations, leaders have to **enable others to act.**"[1]

When God called Moses to lead the children of Israel out of bondage He didn't expect him to lead them by himself. God immediately raised up his sister, Miriam, a prophetess (Exodus 15:20), and his brother Aaron, Moses' spokesman, to serve with him. Joshua, Moses' servant, led the fight against Amalek (Exodus 17:9), even as God was preparing him to lead the army of Israel against the armies in Canaan when they reached the Promised Land. When

Moses ascended to the mountain of God, it was Joshua who accompanied him to the foot of the mountain. God was preparing Joshua to be Moses' successor even before Moses might have realized it.

Yet Moses, Aaron, Miriam, and Joshua were not enough by themselves to lead so great a people to their freedom. When Moses' father-in-law, Jethro, the priest of Midian, met Moses in the wilderness after they had left Egypt, he recognized the impossible task Moses had accepted. Jethro wisely advised Moses that the role he assumed was untenable and one he could not accomplish alone. "Furthermore, you shall select out of all the people able men who fear God, men of truth, those who hate dishonest gain; and you shall place these over them as leaders of thousands, of hundreds, of fifties and of tens" (Exodus 18:21).

The greatest example of the discipleship model is Jesus. Jesus is the Son of God, the Messiah, the Redeemer sent from God, the Creator of all things, the Logos; and yet Jesus Himself gave us the example of shared leadership. Before Jesus came, the prophets and ultimately John the Baptist prepared the way for Him. When he began His ministry, He first selected the twelve (Mark 3:13-19) and later sent out the seventy (Luke 10:1). From the beginning of His ministry, Jesus had a plan of expansion and succession. He ministered to the thousands, the hundreds, and even one on one. Jesus taught His disciples by precept and example, teaching them through real life experiences the mysteries of eternity. The disciples and the seventy were given authority by Jesus and ministered in His name. Before ascending into Heaven, Jesus empowered and commissioned His followers to make disciples of all the nations.

Significant movements are not the result of single individuals. William Wilberforce is often the one who is recognized first among those who led the abolition of slavery movement in England in the

19th century. However the work to change the hearts of the people began much earlier. In the 17th and 18th centuries, English Quakers and evangelical religious groups were already condemning slavery. John and Charles Wesley, George Whitefield, and the leaders of the Great Awakening preached a gospel accessible to all people, equally created in the image of God. John Newton, once a slave ship captain who became a pastor after conversion and writer of numerous hymns including one of today's most popular hymns, *Amazing Grace,* gave leadership to the abolition movement and specifically provided guidance to Wilberforce as a young boy and later when he was a member of the Parliament.

Josiah Wedgwood, famed maker of stunning dinnerware, contributed artistic skills to design the medallion for the British anti-slavery campaign, (Am I not a man, and a brother?). Hannah More, noted author, channeled her literary prowess to produce books, plays, and pamphlets addressing the horrors of slavery. Multiple avenues were used to change the public perception of this evil. A group of prominent British evangelicals were called the Clapham Sect. They were named for one of the leaders John Venn, who was the rector of Clapham in South London. The Clapham Sect, also called the Clapham Circle, included Wilberforce, Henry Thornton, James Stephen, Zachary Macaulay, Hannah More, and others, campaigned for the abolition of slavery both in England and beyond.

> "Leaders know they can't make extraordinary things happen all by themselves. It takes partners, so leaders invest in building spirited and cohesive teams, teams that feel like family. They develop collaborative goals and cooperative relationships with colleagues. They know these relationships are the keys that unlock support."[2]

Jesus spent time praying before He made the decision to select the followers He would entrust with His plan for redemption. His choices were certainly unorthodox. Most leaders having a goal to bring transformation to the world, would have looked for persons of power, influence, brilliance, and a proven track record. Rather than assembling a group of respected religious leaders and political strategists, Jesus poured His life into fishermen and even a despised tax collector. Judea was the center of faith and influence, yet Jesus only selected one disciple from there, Judas. The other eleven were from the backwoods area of Galilee; men often ridiculed for their speech and lack of formal training. Jesus looked at their heart rather than their resume and saw exactly the kind of leaders needed to usher in the Kingdom.

Jim Collins, the author of *Good to Great*, created a research team to learn how a few good companies were not satisfied with their success but pushed to become exemplary organizations. They expected to find companies that set a new direction or strategy that got the workers committed to a new vision. The research revealed a surprising reality.

> "The executives who ignited the transformations from good to great did not first figure out where to drive the bus and then get people to take it there. No, they first got the right people on the bus (and the wrong people off the bus) and then figured out where to drive it. They said in essence, 'Look, I don't really know where we should take the bus. But I know this much: If we get the right people on the bus, the right people in the right seats, and the wrong people off the bus, then we'll figure out how to take it someplace great.'"[3]

These leaders learned some simple truths:

1. "If you begin with, 'who,' rather than 'what,' you can more easily adapt to a changing world.
2. "If you have the right people on the bus, the problem of how to motivate and manage people largely goes away.
3. "If you have the wrong people, it doesn't matter whether you discover the right direction; you still won't have a great company. Great vision without great people is irrelevant."[4]

Trust is the foundation of any relationship. If a leader wishes to build a team that is successful, he or she must clarify the essential values. What are some of the qualifications of a team you wish to assemble? Certainly one must consider integrity, motivation, discipline, cooperation, and competence. Leaders should find the best people available even though you accept the fact that others will recruit them when they succeed. Don't try to convert lazy individuals into hardworking people, but create an environment where those who work hard will thrive and those who are lazy "would either jump or get thrown off the bus."[5]

The Collins researchers found three practical disciplines for being rigorous rather than ruthless.

1. *When in doubt, don't hire—keep looking*. "Those who build great companies understand that the ultimate throttle on growth for any great company is not markets, or technology, or competition, or products. It is one thing above all others: the ability to get and keep enough of the right people."[6]
2. *When you know you need to make a personnel change—act.* "The best people don't need to be managed. Guided,

taught, led—yes, but not tightly managed. We've all experienced or observed the following scenario. We have the wrong person on the bus and we know it. Yet we wait, we delay, we try alternatives, we give a third and fourth chance, we hope that the situation will improve, we invest time in trying to properly manage the person, we build little systems to compensate for his shortcomings, and so forth. But the situation doesn't improve."[7] Two questions that help a leader discern whether the person is the right person for the job are: If given the choice would you hire this person again? If the person came to you and said I'm leaving for another job would you be pleased or disappointed?

3. *Put your best people on your biggest opportunities—not your biggest problems.* "Indeed, one of the crucial elements in taking a company from good to great is somewhat paradoxical. You need executives, on the one hand, who argue and debate—sometimes violently—in pursuit of the best answers, yet, on the other hand, who unify fully behind a decision, regardless of parochial interests."[8]

Not every leader gets to pick the team with whom they will serve, nor does every leader have the authority to get rid of team members who are unproductive. Boards, committees, congregational authority, deacons, elders, and additional structures govern many churches, and other non-profits. When a new pastor arrives, he typically must adjust to the leaders already in place. At times, the new leader may be told he can change the current staff or leadership and build his own team. Don't be too quick to believe that. I have observed that the dismissal of any staff member, regardless of the reason, comes with a cost.

New leaders in any organization need the time to learn the history, values, DNA, heroes, stories, celebrations, and dreams of the institution before making meaningful changes. As trust is built and confidence gained, leaders must build the relationships that facilitate confidence as decisions are made. Every organization has its own written governance that must be followed as well as an unwritten code of conduct that should be observed. Make small changes. As decisions are made, and small wins begin to occur, confidence in the leader increases.

Just as Jesus relied on prayer before assembling His team, prayer is essential as we seek God's plan for the people we are called to lead. A Bible promise that continues to be an encouragement to me as I seek God's leadership is Romans 8:26-27. "In the same way the Spirit also helps our weakness; for we do not know how to pray as we should, but the Spirit Himself intercedes for us with groanings too deep for words; and He who searches the hearts knows what the mind of the Spirit is, because He intercedes for the saints according to the will of God."

The fifth best practice in *The Leadership Challenge* is **encourage the heart.** "The climb to the top is arduous and long. People become exhausted, frustrated, and disenchanted. They're often tempted to give up. Leaders *encourage the heart* of their constituents to carry on. Genuine acts of caring uplifts the spirits and draw people forward."[9]

My wife Sheila and I had the privilege of being part of the founding of a new seminary, The John Leland Center for Theological Studies, in Northern Virginia. Even though the dream was a personal dream that was ours, we soon learned that others throughout the years had a similar passion. One morning as Sheila and I were eating breakfast at a restaurant near the Metro in Northern

Virginia, we began observing all of the different ethnicities and languages of the folks seated around us. God touched our hearts and we wondered how it is possible for us to share the hope of the Gospel with so many different people. It would be practically and financially impossible to build churches for all of these different cultures. Yet we began to realize God's plan all along has been to prepare leaders that others will follow. Our question then became, how do we equip leaders?

As we continued our conversation, Sheila recalled a dream that she had one night when we were still living in Florida. She clearly dreamed of a seminary that was meeting in a church building and was attended by people from numerous ethnic and language groups. At the time of our conversation, I was privileged to be the Senior Pastor of the Columbia Baptist Church in Falls Church, Virginia. For years the church held ten worship services in the church building every Sunday, four in English and six in other languages. The church also had an ESL program (English as a Second Language) with over a hundred participants every semester and a Day Care that enrolled hundreds of children from numerous religious and language backgrounds. In addition, Columbia hosted a Korean Seminary and accommodated classes from Averett University, a Virginia Baptist college.

Washington, D.C., was already the location of several wonderful seminaries from various denominations, but none from a Baptist perspective. We began to engage pastors and denominational leaders about the need for a Baptist seminary in our area and found that others shared the same concern. We began doing feasibility studies and recognized there was a need. We consulted with other seminaries to see if they were interested in beginning a campus in our area and even though there was interest, no school was ready to provide the resources to begin an extension. During that time, five of us with a similar dream attended a Baptist World Alliance meeting in Canada including Sheila and me, two Northern Virginia pastors Dr. Michael Catlett and Dr. Jeff Willetts, and a professor from Argentina, Dr. Daniel Carro. As we discussed the possibility of a Baptist seminary in the DC community, Dr. Carro made the statement, "If we are going to ruin it let's ruin it ourselves." With that rousing challenge to ruin it ourselves, we made a commitment to return home and move forward with the school.

The Leland Center would have never started without the dedicated leadership of dozens of pastors, many who became adjunct or associate professors, and a Board of dedicated volunteers who helped us to raise the money and create the documents essential for such an endeavor. Columbia Baptist Church provided the facilities and early funding. The school received full accreditation with the Association of Theological Schools after eight years and was immediately invited to join the Washington Consortium of Seminaries at the same time. By God's grace, Leland celebrated its 20th anniversary in 2019 and continues to train men and women from multiple ethnicities to be leaders in church life especially in the DC metropolitan area. Some of the volunteers and professors who began with the school in its early days continue to be actively involved in keeping the dream alive.

God brought together the right people to be on the bus for the new institution. As they came together they envisioned a seminary that was Baptist in its heritage but one that welcomed students and partnerships with other Christian institutions. Leland created articulation agreements with other seminaries in the area to share library resources and faculty.

The focus was on preparing leaders for the local church in a multicultural urban environment. From the start Leland hired a small, academically excellent multilingual faculty, who were supported with associate and adjunct faculty with requisite academic credentials who were already living in the area. The decision was made early on that Leland would not purchase a building but would seek existing church facilities that were available during the week as an incubator for training church staff. Since it was highly unlikely that potential students would relocate to DC and dedicate three or more years to theological education, it was decided that the focus was recruiting second career students who attended classes in the evenings, Saturdays, or intensive courses adjusting to the students' available time schedules.

The Leland faculty, students, and volunteers became a family. Even though it has faced the same challenges that all schools and institutions face with an ever-changing culture, hundreds of students have come through the Leland programs and are sharing the hope of Christ within their own calling.

Assembling the right team, whether at the beginning of a new ministry or the reshaping of an existing team over a period of time, is challenging but essential to success.

Leaders should:

- Avoid the first person and always say "we."
- Ask questions, listen, and take advice.
- Enrich the jobs of others.
- Stop talking and start building relationships at staff meetings.
- Strengthen others by increasing self-determination and developing competence.

"Making extraordinary things happen in organizations is hard work. Leaders encourage their followers' hearts to go the distance. They visibly acknowledge people's efforts in pursuit of the common vision. With a thank-you note, a smile, and public praise, they let others know how much they mean to the organization.

Leaders also express pride in the accomplishments of their teams. They make a point of telling the rest of the organization about what the teams have achieved. Celebration is important to a winning team. Leaders find ways to mark accomplishments. They take time out to rejoice in reaching a milestone and to gather spirit and support to continue.

Recognize contributions by showing appreciation for individual excellence, and celebrate the values and victories by creating a spirit of community."[10]

Endnotes

[1] Kouzes and Posner, *The Leadership Challenge*, 20.

[2] James M. Kouzes and Barry Z. Posner, *The Leadership Challenge Workbook*, Third Edition (San Francisco, CA: Jossey-Bass, 2012), 91.

[3] Collins, *Good to Great*, 41.

[4] Ibid., 42.

[5] Ibid., 51.

[6] Ibid., 54.

[7] Ibid., 56.

[8] Ibid., 60.

[9] Kouzes and Posner, *The Leadership Challenge*, 21-22.

[10] Kouzes and Posner, *The Leadership Workbook*, 109.

12
Living With Courage: Facing Opposition, Criticism, and Persecution

"Therefore, since we have so great a cloud of witnesses surrounding us, let us also lay aside every encumbrance and the sin which so easily entangles us, and let us run with endurance the race that is set before us, fixing our eyes on Jesus, the author and perfecter of faith, who for the joy set before Him endured the cross, despising the shame, and has sat down at the right hand of the throne of God. For consider Him who has endured such hostility by sinners against Himself, so that you will not grow weary and lose heart" (Hebrews 12:1-3).

Martin Luther King, Jr. told of the brutal challenge the Civil Rights leaders faced in Alabama. "With the jails filling up and the scorching glare of national disapproval focused on Birmingham, Bull Connor abandoned his posture of nonviolence. The result was an ugliness too well known to Americans and to people all over the world. The newspapers of May 4, 1963, carried pictures of prostrate women, and policemen bending over them with raised clubs;

of children marching up to the bared fangs of police dogs; of the terrible force of pressure hoses sweeping bodies into the streets.

This was the time of our greatest stress, and the courage and conviction of those students and adults made it our finest hour. We did not fight back, but we did not turn back."[1]

On December 1, 1955, Rosa Parks, a seamstress at a local department store in Montgomery, Alabama, was sitting in the "colored" section of a city bus when she was ordered by the bus driver, James Blake, to relinquish her seat for a white man who boarded the bus after the white section was filled. However, on that day Parks came to the place where she had enough of this racial discrimination, and she refused to comply. As a result, Rosa Parks was arrested. Her act of defiance became a symbol of the Civil Rights Movement and her court case ultimately led to a boycott of the Montgomery buses for over a year. Even though her case bogged down in the courts, ultimately the federal lawsuit, Browder v. Gayle, resulted in a November 1956 decision that bus segregation is unconstitutional.

Rosa Parks became a hero to many and received national and even international recognition. Some states have even established Rosa Parks Day. Yet her act of courage also was costly. She lost her job, received numerous death threats, and moved to Detroit where she found a similar job.

Gandhi's example of nonviolent resistance was an inspiration for Martin Luther King, Jr. When King encountered some African students that were in India voicing opposition to the nonviolent approach. King said,

> "We soon discovered that they, like many others, tended to confuse passive resistance with nonresistance. This is completely wrong. True nonviolent resistance is not unrealistic

> submission to an evil power. It is rather a courageous confrontation of evil by the power of love, in the faith that it is better to be the recipient of violence than the inflicter of it, since the latter only multiplies the existence of violence and bitterness in the universe, while the former may develop a sense of shame in the opponent, and thereby bring about a transformation and change of heart."[2]

In a sermon King preached on March 22, 1959, in Montgomery, Alabama, he referred to Gandhi,

> "The world doesn't like people like Gandhi. That's strange, isn't it? They don't like people like Christ; they don't like people like Lincoln. They killed him—this man who had done all of that for India, who gave his life and who mobilized and galvanized 400 million people for independence... One of his fellow Hindus felt that he was too favorable toward the Moslems, felt he was giving in too much for the Moslems... Here was the man of nonviolence, falling at the hands of a man filled with hate."[3]

Nine years later the same fate fell to King.

Emergent leadership requires courage. Not always does change require prison, beatings, and executions, but it will always require valor. William Wilberforce's life was threatened many times because of his opposition to slavery. "Wilberforce was a tiny, frail man; for him, being brave entailed being very brave indeed. During his testimony in the House of Commons in 1792, he named a vicious Bristol slave-ship captain who had flogged to death a fifteen-year-old African girl. As a result of the evidence Wilberforce presented, this Captain Kimber was put on trial for murder. He was acquitted through what seemed an outrageous miscarriage of justice—another painful loss for the abolitionists."[4] Kimber demanded a public apology from Wilberforce and a government position, which Wilberforce ignored. Afterward, Kimber made numerous threats against Wilberforce.

On one occasion, Thomas Clarkson, a fellow abolitionist and friend of Wilberforce, met a man on a stagecoach who presented to him a dark and hitherto unknown aspect of Wilberforce's character. "'He is no doubt a great philanthropist in public,' the man allowed, 'but I happen to know a little of his private history and can assure you that he is a cruel husband and beats his wife.' Wilberforce was, of course, still a bachelor at the time—and how lucky for his wife."[5]

At times courageous leadership may necessitate standing up to the bully who reminds the leader that "we have always done it this way before," or it may be a life and death decision like Martin Luther who stood before Emperor Charles V to defend what he had taught and written and was reported to have responded, "Here I stand, I can do no other, God help me. Amen."

When I made the decision to follow in my father's footsteps and enter the ministry, he gave me some advice that I continue to carry with me decades later. He said, "When people criticize you, if they knew the whole story they probably would not have." He continued, "When people praise you, if they knew the whole story they probably would not have." His warning then was to pay little attention to either criticism or praise.

When Moses was seeking to bring freedom to his enslaved fellow Hebrews, he faced opposition from the Egyptian Pharaoh, the slave masters and even the Egyptian army. Certainly Moses expected those clashes. He was also unsurprised at the opposition of the sons of Amalek who fought against him at Rephidim and the other armies he faced during the exodus. However Moses' greatest disappointment may have been the opposition of his own people like the rebellion of Korah (Numbers 16) and especially the murmuring of his own brother and sister, Aaron and Miriam (Numbers 12) in a clash over power.

Nehemiah constantly faced opposition from Tobiah, Sanballat, and Geshem as he attempted to rebuild the walls of Jerusalem (Nehemiah 6). The Apostle Paul endured persecution from the Romans, even though he was a Roman citizen, and from his Jewish brothers, even though he had been a leader as a Pharisee. Even Christian leaders criticized Paul. In Philippians 1:15, Paul alluded to the envy and strife of other preachers while he was a prisoner chained to Roman guards. Jesus was delivered up for crucifixion by the Jews and executed by the Romans. On the night of Jesus arrest, he was betrayed by one of His own disciples and another of His closest followers, Peter, denied even knowing Jesus. That same night His other followers fled when He needed their supporting presence the most.

Opposition didn't stop King, or Moses, or Nehemiah, or Paul, or Jesus. Peter, in a moment of weakness, denied Jesus but later became a courageous leader of the early church. Later he wrote about his own suffering as an encouragement to other Christ followers, "Beloved, do not be surprised at the fiery ordeal among you, which comes upon you for your testing, as though some strange thing were happening to you; but to the degree that you share the sufferings of Christ, keep on rejoicing, so that also at the revelation of His glory you may rejoice with exultation" (1 Peter 4:12-13).

When Paul preached in Ephesus miracles took place and the "word of the Lord was growing mightily and prevailing" (Acts

19:20). While the gospel brought freedom to some, it caused a disturbance among others.

"For a man named Demetrius, a silversmith, who made silver shrines of Artemis, was bringing no little business to the craftsmen; these he gathered together with the workmen of similar trades, and said, 'Men, you know that our prosperity depends upon this business. You see and hear that not only in Ephesus, but in almost all of Asia, this Paul has persuaded and turned away a considerable number of people, saying that gods made with hands are no gods at all. Not only is there a danger that this trade of ours fall into disrepute, but also that the temple of the great goddess Artemis be regarded as worthless and that she whom all of Asia and the world worship will even be dethroned from her magnificence.' When they heard this and were filled with rage, they began crying out, saying, 'Great is Artemis of the Ephesians!'" (Acts 19:24-28).

Why should we be surprised when those who benefit from oppression resist those who oppose oppressive systems? Freedom for the enslaved brings exposure and negative consequences to those who were the oppressors. Human slavery was an important part of the economic equation of England before slavery was abolished. Slavery was tolerated and even supported in America because it was thought to be essential to farming. Slave owners used Scripture to justify their cruel actions and churches often remained silent for fear of retaliation from those benefiting from slavery. Some attempted to mollify their behavior by creating churches for slaves or some justified their actions by pretentious acts of generosity or kindness to slaves while at the same time owning humans as though they were merely tools.

When a leader seeks to bring change, whether it is against systemic evil or a pastor attempting to turn around a declining congregation, that leader should expect opposition.

However, not all resistance is unprovoked. I think back to my own experiences and remember too often the very action I thought was needed may have hurt rather than helped. At times it may have been because my ideas were wrong, or the timing may not have been right, or the team had not been adequately prepared for the action I suggested. I am grateful that in each of my ministry opportunities, there have always been wise partners who confronted me when I was wrong. Transformational leaders do not serve by themselves, as we discussed in the previous chapter, but must be part of a team where there is the encouragement for honest dialogue and disagreements encouraged when expressed in a spirit of humility.

> "Even though we urge every leader to experiment, take risks, and learn from the accompanying mistakes, we know that many learning experiences can be very stressful and painful. Falling down when skiing can result in injury. Failure to achieve the expected results from an innovation can set you back. And despite the overwhelmingly positive emotions associated with personal best cases, we can't overlook the fact that they were filed with stress. Although 95% of the cases were described as exciting, about 20% of leaders also called the experiences frustrating, and approximately 15% said that their experiences aroused fear or anxiety.
>
> Disruptive change demands significant commitment and sacrifice, but the positive feelings associated with the forward progress generate momentum that enables you to ride out the storm."[6]

Although leadership requires courage and endurance, transformational leadership is worth the cost when a person knows he or she is right in the center of God's kingdom assignment. "Consider it all joy, my brethren, when you encounter various trials, knowing that the testing of your faith produces endurance. And let endurance have its perfect result, so that you may be perfect and complete, lacking in nothing" (James 1:2-4).

At the beginning of this chapter, we find one of the most important scriptures that continues to guide me as I seek to follow God's leadership. Hebrews 12:1-3 reminds us: we are not alone, God has placed us in a race that requires endurance, our focus must be on Jesus and not on our circumstances, and the race ultimately ends in the joy that awaits us.

Endnotes

[1] Carson, *The Autobiography of Martin Luther King, Jr.,* 208-209.

[2] Ibid., 130.

[3] Ibid., 132.

[4] Metaxas, *Amazing Grace*, 156.

[5] Ibid., 157-158.

[6] Kouzes and Posner, *The Leadership Challenge*, 205.

Part 3

Leading Systemic Changes: Implementing Practices and Legislation That Insure the Enduring Effect of Social Change

If you ask historians who is the person most responsible for the protection of religious freedom in our U.S. Constitution, they will probably reply James Madison. If we asked Madison he should say John Leland and the Virginia Baptists. Leland actually had more support than Madison for election to the House of Representatives but the two of them met together and Leland promised to step back from the race if Madison promised to include a provision for religious freedom in the new Constitution. They agreed and Madison kept his word and wrote the protection in the first amendment.

In Orange County, Virginia, at the Leland-Madison Memorial Park, there is a monument dedicated to the contribution of the Virginia Baptist pastor, John Leland, who led in the effort for religious freedom. Beneath the relief of John Leland, the monument reads,

> "Elder John Leland courageous leader of the Baptist doctrine, ardent advocate of the principles of democracy, vindicator of separation of church and state. Near this spot in 1788, Elder John Leland and James Madison, the father of the American Constitution held a significant interview, which resulted in the adoption of the Constitution by Virginia. Then Madison, a member of Congress from Orange presented the First Amendment to the Constitution guaranteeing religious liberty, free speech and a free press. This satisfied Leland and his Baptist followers."

> "Leland is known not only for his fiery sermons and evangelical zeal, but also for his opposition to slavery and his advocacy of strict separation between government and religion. Leland preached freedom in all aspects of life, exhorting his listeners to be free from sin, to oppose slavery and free others from physical bondage, and to be free from the 'spiritual tyranny' of state-established religion."[1]

When my wife and I joined with a group from Northern Virginia to begin a Baptist seminary, we suggested only one name for the school and that was John Leland, who ironically was opposed to seminaries. We named the school for him because of his strong leadership supporting the abolition of slavery, his role in the establishment of religious freedom, and his work as a church planter and evangelist. Leland was born in Massachusetts and served pastorates in Virginia from 1775-1791. He left Virginia the year the *Bill of Rights* was ratified and after a strong anti-slavery sermon that he preached.

Not even John Leland's passion and convicting sermons were enough to bring the protection for religious freedom by themselves. Systemic changes require new practices, reframing narratives, and legislation to ensure that old oppression will not continue to restrict freedom. John Leland knew that verbal approval by James Madison and the framers would never last more than a generation. He and others with him made sure that this freedom was spelled out in the Constitution.

Emergent leaders must keep future generations in mind as they work for justice. Wilberforce didn't settle for platitudes and resolutions by the Parliament. He fought until slavery was abolished, a practice still restricted in Britain. Martin Luther King, Jr. did not just depend on rousing crowds and public gatherings to voice support for Blacks, he gave his life leading others to abolish Jim Crow laws and overturn racial segregation.

Leland wrote,

> "The notion of a Christian commonwealth should be exploded forever...Government should protect every man in thinking and speaking freely, and see that one does not abuse another. The liberty I contend for is more than toler-

ation. The very idea of toleration is despicable; it supposes that some have a pre-eminence above the rest to grant indulgence, whereas all should be equally free, Jews, Turks, Pagans, and Christians."[2]

Systemic change requires advocacy, dismissing false narratives, building collaboration and creating institutions that will not only usher in justice but also protect future generations from oppressive practices. Christians and other religious groups in America might be suffering the same persecution that is found in so much of the world if not for leaders like John Leland.

13 Advocates for Change

"Pure and undefiled religion in the sight of our God and Father is this: to visit orphans and widows in their distress, and keep oneself unstained by the world" (James 1:27).

If oppressive laws are overcome, it will be because of the leadership of folks like William Wilberforce and Martin Luther King, Jr., who are willing to work toward the shifting of public opinion and the fight to eliminate unjust systems that continue to perpetrate the subjugation of minorities. One contemporary leader is Dr. Bob Fu, the Founder and President of ChinaAid.

"America Stand Up for Religious Freedom!"

I do not know anyone who does a better job of advocacy for religious freedom than Bob Fu. When Bob arrived in the United States in 1997 as a fugitive from China, he would have never dreamed that one day he and his family would be forced to leave for a safe house in this country because a threat had been made on his life. Guo Wengui, a billionaire Chinese, in the U.S. on a tourist visa and living in a Manhattan penthouse, built a following as a blogger under the alias "Miles Kwok." Beginning in January of 2020, he began to target Bob Fu and posted a message on YouTube openly calling on his followers to kill Bob Fu and others he listed on a "global kill cheaters" campaign, claiming Bob to be a communist spy.

In late September of 2020, agitators showed up in front of Bob's house every day as a reminder of the serious nature of the warning. Local law officials and the FBI moved Bob and his family to a safe house for their protection. His situation is another reminder that Communist China tries to silence dissidents even if they live in Midland, Texas.

This is not the first time Bob and Heidi have been targeted by the Chinese. They both became Christians after the Tiananmen Square massacre when Chinese soldiers killed innocent students in 1989. Bob believed he could work within the government framework and still share the gospel, but he soon learned the Communist Party would not tolerate his beliefs. During the day, Bob taught English to future Communist leaders and in the evening he trained leaders for the illegal church. Bob called himself "a double agent," that later provided the name for his excellent autobiography, *God's Double Agent.*[3] Ultimately Bob and Heidi both were sent to prison for their activities.

When they were released from prison it wasn't long before Heidi became pregnant with their first child even though they had not received permission from the government to bear a child. Their only option to keep from aborting the baby was to flee China. After a courageous and miraculous escape from China they arrived in Hong Kong where they learned they could not get a visa for the U.S. The clock was ticking because Hong Kong was on the verge of Britain transferring control of Hong Kong to China. Just after Heidi gave birth to their first child and days before the transition, Bob and Heidi were at McDonalds where a reporter from ABC News with Peter Jennings randomly interviewed them. He asked Bob about his opinion of the impending change in Hong Kong's transition.

Bob boldly responded, "Actually I'm a religious dissident from China, and my family will certainly be arrested again for our Christian religious beliefs unless the United States government will act on our behalf." He continued, "The countdown to the handover is a countdown to our imprisonment. **Please America, stand up for religious freedom."**[4]

Bob's plea spread like wildfire across America and resulted in a letter from President Bill Clinton telling the U.S. Consulate in Hong Kong to let the Fu family come to the U.S.

It would have been easy for Bob and Heidi to enjoy the freedoms of life in the U.S. and never look back. Yet their love for Christ and for their homeland motivated Bob to become one of the leading voices in America for religious freedom in China. Bob has made friends among faith leaders of all religions and has also become a friend to Members of Congress and leaders of four Administrations including several Presidents. I have heard prominent Americans speak of Bob's integrity, courage, and humility. He and I joined a small group who met with Vice President Pence to share our concerns that human rights issues in China are worse now than any time since the Cultural Revolution. We spoke about the atrocities against the Uyghur Muslims of China and the Falun Gong as well as the increased persecution of Christians.

Debra Fikes and the Midland Ministerial Alliance became friends with Bob and worked with Mid-Cities Church and others to relocate the family to Midland where he would be much safer than in Philadelphia. Bob began to serve as an Associate Pastor at

Mid-Cities Church while he continued to do advocacy work in D.C., as well as the U.N. and training house church pastors and human rights lawyers in China.

In April 2006, Fu invited seven Chinese human rights activists to Washington, D.C. During the visit, they met with President Bush at the White House. The group included the prominent Chinese human rights attorney, Li Baiguang and Chinese pastor Wang Yi. In 2017, just a couple of weeks after the national Prayer Breakfast in D.C. that Li attended, we were saddened by the news that Baiguang had died in a Chinese hospital of liver failure. In a Reuters article by Christian Shepherd, on February 26, 2018, Li's death was described as suspicious because of his good health and since he had been healthy and never drank alcohol. Former Congressman Frank Wolf said he and Bob Fu met with Li just a week before he died and he showed no signs of illness. Also on December 30, 2019, Bob's friend Wang Yi was sentenced to nine years in prison. He was the pastor of the Early Rain Covenant Church and had been arrested a year earlier with dozens of other church leaders.

Bob knows the cost that comes to those who stand up to an oppressive government like China. Li Baiguang and Wang Yi are only two of a long list of friends of Bob Fu who have suffered and continue to suffer for their faith. What the Uyghur people in Northwest China are experiencing in China is the Holocaust of our day. The plight of Christians and other religious minorities are not far behind. Under the leadership of President Xi Jinping, the Chinese Communist Party seeks to control all aspects of life. Internet firewalls are built to keep information away from their own citizens. Prisons are filled with good people who seek only to live lives of peace and prosperity.

Bob has been confronted with the two temptations of being silenced by evil people as well as being seduced by powerful people. While some bask in the favor of Presidents and Senators, accommodating the leaders' agendas for a photo op, or withdrawing out of fear from engagement with injustice, Bob stands strong, honest, courageous, and humble.

Bob's statement to the ABC reporter in Hong Kong needs to be heard today. **"Please America, stand up for religious freedom."** Stand up to the tyranny of China. Stop allowing our government officials who leave office to work for law firms that support companies controlled by the Chinese Communist Party. Stop buying products from companies that benefit from the forced labor of prisoners in China. Stop taking our religious freedom in the U.S. for granted.

One day while I was the pastor of First Baptist Church in Midland, Texas, I received a call from Congressman Frank Wolf of Virginia who asked me what it would take to wake up the church in America to the persecution of Christians globally. Shortly after that conversation Michael Horowitz, a prominent attorney from the D.C. community came to Midland and spoke with me about the urgency of the Western church to respond to the persecution of Christians. Both spoke how Bob Fu and ChinaAid were models of engagement with the persecuted in China. Our organization, 21Wilberforce was born from those conversations.

Michael Horowitz said, "The Chinese regime understands that the spread of religious faith and a principle-based legal system in China threatens its very survival as nothing else does. As the person who defends, defines and inspires the tens of million brave house church Christians of China, and quietly supports China's human rights attorneys, Bob Fu is thus a critical history-shaper for generations to come."[5]

Advocacy is essential to confronting injustice and creating legal systems that protect victims and insure others will not be affected by continued oppressive behavior. Bob Fu is one of the most effective advocates I know.

In a statement printed in the Midland Telegram-Reporter on October 11, 2020, U.S. Congressman Chris Smith wrote, "I am deeply concerned that since late September, Pastor Bob Fu, founder of the nonprofit ChinaAid, and his family have been the targets of outrageous slander, libel and intimidation by suspected members of the Chinese Communist Party, and their enablers, and are at grave risk of serious bodily harm. They have been forced to flee their home in Midland, Texas, after protestors in chartered buses arrived at their home. Pastor Fu and his family are currently under police protection.

"The Chinese Communist Party (CCP) hates Pastor Bob Fu—and other Chinese human rights activists living in the United States and elsewhere in the world—and are employing the big lie against Bob Fu in much the same way they do in China."[6]

Congressman Smith is the former chairman of the House Foreign Affairs Human Rights Subcommittee as well as the chair of the Congressional-Executive China Commission—and now serving as Ranking Member on both those panels. He added, "I have been a member of Congress for forty years and attest that Bob Fu is one of the most prayerful, dedicated, disciplined, wise and effective champions for human rights that I have ever met."[7]

Bob Fu's commitment to bringing the atrocities committed by the Communist Chinese Party to public attention is clearly demonstrated by his tireless and bold pursuit of doing the work of advocacy on behalf of the persecuted, even though he knew he would become a target of the CCP. His testimony before Congress, the Administration, the State Department, and even the United Nations forced the cruelties of the Chinese government to become impossible to ignore for the U.S. government.

Congressman Smith said, "At my request and invitation, Pastor Fu gave expert testimony at thirteen separate official congressional hearings (see list below) I've chaired on the Chinese Communist Party's pervasive harassment and persecution of religious believers of all faiths.

Together, we have jointly appeared at press conferences and worked on Chinese human rights legislation.

Members of Congress on both sides of the aisle frequently turn to Pastor Fu for guidance, insight and direction."[8]

"Pastor Fu gave expert testimony at thirteen separate official congressional hearings I've chaired":

1. China's War on Christianity and Other Religious Faiths
2. Dissidents Who Have Suffered for Human Rights in China: A Look Back and A Look Forward
3. Religion With "Chinese Characteristics": Persecution and Control in Xi Jinping's China
4. Protecting Religious Freedom: U.S. Efforts to Hold Accountable Countries of Particular Concern
5. Their Daughters Appeal to Beijing: "Let Our Fathers Go!"
6. Guo Feixiong and Freedom of Expression in China
7. Chen Guangcheng and Gao Zhisheng: Human Rights in China
8. Continued Human Rights Attacks on Families in China

9. Chen Guangcheng: His Case, Cause, Family, and Those Who are Helping Him
10. Recent Developments in History of the Chen Guangcheng Case
11. The Case and Treatment of Prominent Human Rights Lawyer Gao Zhisheng
12. One Year After the Nobel Peace Prize Award to Liu Xiaobo: Conditions for Political Prisoners and Prospects for Political Reform
13. The U.N. Commission on Human Rights: Protector or Accomplice?[9]

Systemic changes require advocacy. If slavery was going to be overthrown in England, Wilberforce knew laws had to be changed. If segregation was to be abolished in the southern states of the U.S., Martin Luther King, Jr. knew discriminating laws had to be stricken from the books.

Overcoming oppressive systems, laws, and practices require emergent leaders who are not involved for selfish benefits, rather those who are willing to pay a price as they engage forces of evil with weapons of peace. The leaders of the Civil Rights Movement in America during the 60s and 70s modeled this approach.

Martin Luther King, Jr. was quoted in the New York Times, February 24, 1956, describing the situation of the bus boycott in Montgomery, Alabama. His statement came just weeks after he and his family escaped the bombing of his house.

> "There are those who would try to make of this a hate campaign. This is not war between the white and the Negro but a conflict between justice and injustice. This is bigger than the Negro race revolting against the white. We are seeking

to improve not the Negro of Montgomery but the whole of Montgomery.

If we are arrested every day if we are exploited every day. If we are trampled over every day, don't ever let anyone pull you so low as to hate them. We must use the weapon of love. We must have compassion and understanding for those who hate us. We must realize so many people are taught to hate us that they are not totally responsible for their hate. But we stand in life at midnight, we are always on the threshold of a new dawn."[10]

King and the leaders of the Civil Rights Movement taught us that advocacy for justice requires multiple approaches. In Montgomery, they hit the economy of the city through an extended boycott of the city buses. In Mississippi, they fought against unjust laws that kept Blacks from registering to vote. In Selma, they used courageous nonviolent marches even when confronted by cruel brutality.

Some folks thought King's participation in the NAACP in Alabama at the same time he was Vice President of the Alabama Council on Human Relations created inconsistency. He responded,

"This question betrayed an assumption that there was only one approach to the solution of the race problem. On the contrary, I felt that both approaches were necessary. Through education we seek to change attitudes and internal feelings (prejudice, hate, etc.); through legislation and court orders we seek to regulate behavior. Anyone who starts out with the conviction that the road to racial justice is only one lane wide will inevitably create a traffic jam and make the journey infinitely longer."[11]

MLK and his colleagues faced continuous challenges but also won important battles. In 1960, King was arrested in Montgomery because of the sit-ins at segregated lunch counters that drew national attention. The authorities sought to make an example of King. He was indicted for perjury and openly announced he was facing at least ten years in prison.

> "This case was tried before an all-white Southern jury. All of the State's witnesses were white. The judge and the prosecutor were white. The courtroom was segregated. Passions were inflamed. Feelings ran high. The press and other communications media were hostile. Defeat seemed certain, and we in the freedom struggle braced ourselves for the inevitable. There were two men among us who persevered with the conviction that it was possible, in this context, to marshal facts and law and thus win vindication. These men were, our lawyers—Negro lawyers from the North: William Ming of Chicago and Hubert Delaney from New York.
>
> They brought to the courtroom wisdom, courage and a highly developed art of advocacy; but most important, they brought the lawyers' indomitable determination to win. After a trial of three days, by the sheer strength of their legal arsenal, they overcame the most vicious Southern taboos festering in a virulent and inflamed atmosphere and they persuaded an all-white jury to accept the word of a Negro over that of white men. The jury, after a few hours of deliberation, returned a verdict of acquittal."[12]

An historic win for the movement came on March 15, 1965, in a speech made by President Lyndon Johnson to a joint session of Congress.

> "Johnson made one of the most eloquent, unequivocal, and passionate pleas for human rights ever made by a President of the United States. He revealed an amazing understanding of the depth and dimension of the problem of racial justice. His tone and his delivery were sincere. He rightly praised the courage of the Negro for awakening the conscience of the nation. He declared that the national government must by law insure every Negro his full rights as a citizen. When he signed the measure (voting bill), the President announced that, 'Today is a triumph for freedom as huge as any victory that's ever been won on any battlefield. Today we strike away the last major shackle of fierce and ancient bonds.'"[13]

We need advocates not just for the powerful but especially for the vulnerable, the voiceless. Advocacy is not just the work of lobbyists working in the state or national capitols. Effective change comes as a result of effective attorneys, courageous pastors, clever strategists, honorable politicians, and bold citizens of all backgrounds taking small and large expressions of support for justice against injustice for as long as it takes to bring about systemic changes.

Bob Fu continues to stand up to a cruel foreign power. King fought against unjust laws in his own country. Earlier we learned how Tillie Burgin took the church out of the church buildings and brought the hope of Christ to people where they lived. What is the injustice in your community that discriminates against the voiceless? Who are the ones working to bring about change? What can you do to join with them to announce freedom to the captives and deliverance to the oppressed? Movements led by charismatic leaders like King will never bring about change unless grassroots activists at the local level rally around the cause.

Endnotes

[1] (John E. Ferguson, Jr., *John Leland*, The First Amendment Encyclopedia, the article was originally published in 2009, Ferguson is a senior lecturer of Business Law and Ethics at Utah State University.)

[2] John Leland, "A Chronicle of His Time in Virginia," *The Writings of the Later Elder John Leland*, published in 1845.

[3] Bob Fu, *God's Double Agent* (Grand Rapids, MI: Baker Publishing Group, 2013).

[4] Ibid., 245.

[5] The prior information about Bob Fu was taken from an Op Ed I (Randel Everett) wrote for the Midland Telegram-Reporter, October 11, 2020.

[6] Statement from Congressman Chris Smith in a guest Op Ed in the Midland Telegram-Reporter, October 11, 2020.

[7] Statement from Congressman Chris Smith in a guest Op Ed in the Midland Telegram-Reporter, October 11, 2020.

[8] Ibid.

[9] Congressman Smith Op Ed

[10] Carson, *The Autobiography of Martin Luther King, Jr.*, 81.

[11] Ibid., 49.

[12] Ibid., 118.

[13] Ibid., 288.

14

Partners in Collaboration

Having spent most of my life as a pastor, I am ashamed to admit that during the past several decades the church in America has been involved in a mindless pursuit of growth. Leaders were validated according to the size of the congregations they led. Churches competed with each other for members, funds, recognition, and influence. Pastors became celebrities; worship became entertainment; pulpits were removed from the "stage;" the countdown for the show to begin was announced and the room grew dark and the stage was lit with spectacular lighting. On special occasions entertainers were paid thousands of dollars to appear and sing, "I'd rather have Jesus than silver or gold."

Churches that achieved successful growth became models for other churches so they too could prosper. Pastors were tempted to avoid controversial subjects for fear of alienating potential members. And while we were leading our churches to grow, hunger, poverty, racism, crime, and other unjust practices flourished. Why should we be surprised if Gen Z is rejecting the church in growing numbers and polls are showing a sharp increase in the number of folks who claim no religious interest? What will happen after the pandemic? Will people return to the church buildings? Will the emphasis shift away from us to Christ and to others? Will we finally hear the cries of our brothers and sisters who are suffering under religious persecution that are asking, "Where is the Church in the West?"

I do not believe God's purpose for our lives is to make us rich or powerful, even though some faithful Christ followers are good stewards of opportunities and resources God has provided for them. God has called us to serve. I continue to return to Micah 6:8, "...And what does the Lord require of you but to do justice, to love kindness, and to walk humbly with your God?" Working for justice is not a task any of us can do alone. We must work with others who share our burden.

One of my favorite sayings is "Lighthouses do not compete. There are not enough of them." The church will never "over serve" the needs of the community. What can happen if churches unite to resist evil in a community, come together to be sure that the issues of hunger and homelessness are addressed, stand together to resist racism? If God's people are not growing in righteousness then the church is not well, regardless of the size of the crowd.

Slavery may have never been outlawed in England without the Great Awakening. The preaching of George Whitfield united the colonies in a time of repentance with men, women, and children of all races coming to Christ. Would the action of Virginia Baptists and Pastor John Leland have ever brought religious freedom to the new Constitution without the Awakening? Other great movements are the results of churches inspired to "Do justice, love mercy, and to walk humbly with God." It was the Black Church in America that forced our nation to deal with the discrimination of segregation.

Positive social change will not happen as long as good people compete with each other for recognition. Collaboration is essential for progress. Collaboration begins among like-minded people but ultimately must reach out to groups who may differ from each other on some issues but unite around common goals. When members of all faith groups work together for religious freedom, and various political parties agree to stand together against racism, and when communities say every child in our city will receive at least one nutritious meal every day, injustice will be overcome.

As God called me to be a pastor, our son, Jeremy, knows that God called him to serve the poor. God has opened some excellent doors for him to participate with others in bringing real change to communities of concern. About a dozen years ago, Jeremy began conversations with a few others about the tragic situation in Texas related to children who do not have access to nutritious meals. In a poor neighborhood where he and his family lived, he witnessed children looking for food in a trash container. These conversations led to the founding of Texas Hunger Initiative at Baylor University.

Jeremy began with the assumption that surely there is enough food in Texas for everyone to be fed. He also realized that even though many groups around the state were committed to feeding the hungry, the problem appeared to be becoming more urgent. One of the first things his small organization did was to do a study of every county in Texas and learn of the needs and resources related to hunger. They recognized government provisions like the SNAP food program, church kitchens for the poor, effective Food Banks, and other excellent programs with dedicated leaders. No one program or one group could solve a problem of this scope. The crisis required public and private partnerships.

> "The Texas Hunger Initiative is a multi-disciplinary project dedicated to ending hunger through research and innovation and committed to strengthening public policy to ad-

dress domestic food insecurity." Jeremy Everett, founder and executive director of THI, said, "The organization was founded on a realization that complex societal problems like hunger and poverty need solutions that leverage the resources of the public and private sectors, faith-based organizations and university researchers"[1] (Baylor.edu/texashunger).

The initiative's broad-based approach includes a dispersed staff that can observe problems first-hand to come up with evidence-based solutions.

'We now have field staff throughout the state working in a learning-lab capacity. The average researcher might have his own laboratory. Our laboratory is the state of Texas,' Everett said.

'We want to leave society better than we found it,' he said. 'Our faculty and students want to be engaged in research and evaluation, but they also want to see how that makes a difference in a young child getting access to food who previously wouldn't have had it without that engagement.'

Jeremy wrote, 'Poverty and food insecurity are challenges that go beyond the capabilities of any one agency or private firm. We play a vital role in addressing these issues by helping to create partnerships between public programs and private organizations, but our work is only possible through the support of our corporate and foundation partners.'"[2]

THI has grown into a broader center renamed the Baylor Collaborative on Hunger and Poverty. When the pandemic of 2020 hit, the ones who were most vulnerable with little resources for nutritious meals were hardest hit. How do children living in rural communities across the U.S., who are dependent on the school meal programs, receive food when schools are closed? THI already had a tested model ready to respond to the problem. It required the collaboration of the federal government, corporations, and local volunteers to pull it off.

The Collaborative worked with the U.S. Department of Agriculture, McLane Global, and PepsiCo to deliver food to school kids who depend on free and reduced lunches, focusing on remote areas.

"We are all concerned about the challenges in large cities, but imagine if you live in the Iberia Parish in Louisiana or the Nome Borough in Alaska," McLane Global Chairman Denton McLane said during a Friday Press Conference at the White House. "So often, the Mom and Dad can't get to the school to pick up meals. That's about to change, and change for the better."

PepsiCo donated $1 million to the Baylor Collaborative on Hunger and Poverty for the program, and McLane Global was tasked to source, package, and ship out boxes that contain two weeks' worth of shelf-stable food. The program, dubbed *Emergency Meals to You*, was based on a program Baylor launched in summer 2019, where they worked with around twenty school districts and served about 480,000 meals and snacks to kids in rural East and West Texas that wouldn't have otherwise received them.

The opportunity and need created by the pandemic were greater than they even imagined. "Our goal was to have 100,000 kids in the program and serve 1 million meals for them per week, but in one state alone we've already had interest from, essentially, over 100,000 kids," Everett said. So the Collaborative had to figure out how to scale up more robustly. The Collaborative accepted the challenge and called in key public and private partners to assist, ultimately growing the program from its origins of delivering 500,000 meals to 4,000 students in Texas only to serving a total of 38,783,860 meals to 270,488 children in 44 states and Puerto Rico.

The Baylor initiative to address hunger in Texas is an example of the power of partnerships. A quote attributed to President Harry Truman reminds us of a great truth, "You can accomplish anything in life, provided that you do not mind who gets the credit." Charismatic leaders may be able to inspire, but for meaningful systemic changes to take place, a grass roots movement is required.

Collaboration begins with obvious partners. The organization I serve, 21Wilberforce, works for international religious freedom. I became passionate about the foundational importance of religious freedom for people of all faiths because that was a core historical belief of my denominational affiliation with Baptists. The Ethics and Religious Liberty Commission (ERLC) of the Southern Baptist Convention published twenty quotes from Baptists on religious liberty. I will highlight four of them:

- In 1611, Thomas Helwys wrote, "For men's religion to God is between God and themselves. The king shall not answer for it. Neither may the king be judge between God and man. Let them be heretics, Turks, Jews or whatsoever it appertains not to the earthly power to punish them in the least measure."
- In 1773, Isaac Backus wrote, "Religious matters are to be separated from the jurisdiction of the state, not because they are beneath the interests of the state but, quite to the contrary, because they are too high and holy and thus are beyond the competence of the state."

- John Leland, who was a primary influence on James Madison for the First Amendment, wrote in 1791, "If government can answer for individuals at the day of judgment, let men be controlled by it in religious matters; otherwise let men be free."
- George W. Truett, President of the Baptist World Alliance and Pastor of the First Baptist Church of Dallas, wrote in 1920, "Baptists have one consistent record concerning liberty throughout all their long and eventful history. They have never been a party to oppression of conscience. They have forever been the unwavering champions of liberty, both religious and civil."[3]

Because of my background as a Baptist and having been involved in the work of the Baptist World Alliance for twenty-five years, it was only natural that 21Wilberforce would reach out to the BWA as a global partner for this issue. In 2020, the BWA and 21Wilberforce entered into an agreement that gave us access to a grassroots network of 47 million Baptists in 126 different countries. If our concern is for religious freedom and against the perilous opposite, religious persecution, we needed to hear from folks living in countries of concern about the challenges and resources related to this cause.

However, the work for justice is not just coalitions of fraternal partners. We must also seek an alliance with those who share our concern yet who may have very different perspectives on other issues. Our organization recognized the need for relationships with other faith groups and even those without any faith affiliation, who share our passion for religious freedom. One of our primary partners is the International Religious Freedom Roundtable in Washington, D.C.

The IRF Roundtable offer simple and elegant ways to bring people together—despite deep theological and political differences—and build mutual understanding, respect, trust and reliance among groups, citizens and governments. They have proven to be effective at building consensus-based coalitions that drive multi-faith engagement actions that impact public policy to advance religious freedom for everyone, everywhere.

Our partnership with the Roundtable has allowed us to build friendships of trust and respect for individuals and groups who differ significantly from us at times on other issues but have become faithful partners standing with those experiencing religious persecution globally.

International religious persecution is a global existential crisis that affects men, women, and children of all faiths. Attempting to expose perpetrators of these offenses whether they are authoritarian governments, radical religious groups, or single individuals inflicting violence against others with whom they disagree, requires the partnerships of faith communities, government agencies like USCIRF (United States Commission on Religious Freedom), and NGO's who work together for a common cause.

What specific injustice keeps you awake at night? Is it religious persecution, hunger, homelessness, racism, protection for the unborn, plight of the immigrants, care for the elderly, sex trafficking, foster children, or orphans? Addressing these issues requires more than just an occasional prayer (as important as that is), or an annual donation. Systemic injustice requires the dedication and sacrifice of coalitions of likeminded individuals and organizations who will pursue justice with the passion and sacrifice of Wilberforce and MLK. Laws may need to be changed, violators must be exposed, and false narratives corrected. In the next chapter, we will be reminded of a woman who helped set the record straight about slavery.

Endnotes

[1] Website for THI: www.Baylor.edu/texashunger.

[2] Baylor website, www.Baylor.edu, Accessed September 26, 2019.

[3] *"20 Quotes form Baptists on Religious Liberty*, by Joe Carter, June 9, 2016, ERLC.

15 Changing the Narrative

False narratives disguising injustice and satisfying those who profit from them often support unjust systems. For most of human history, slavery was not only tolerated but it was actually promoted as an essential element of the global economy. Good people too often wish to be sheltered from the harsh realities of religious persecution, human trafficking, hunger, mass migrations of communities fleeing from ethnic or religious cleansing, war, and natural disasters; while clinging to a myopic illusion that people are basically decent. How often we pacify our indifference with the deception that evil doesn't exist if it is not experienced personally.

I have stood before the quotation of the German pastor Martin Niemoller on permanent display in the United States Holocaust Museum and pondered what is the injustice we are ignoring today?

First they came for the socialists, and I did not speak out—because I was not a socialist.
Then they came for the trade unionists, and I did not speak out—because I was not a trade unionist.
Then they came for the Jews, and I did not speak out—because I was not a Jew.

Then they came for me—and there was no one left to speak for me.[1]

During the 19th century, the conversation in Britain and in the U.S. often reflected a very positive idea about slavery. Some believed that slaves actually were better off than when they were living in their former villages of Africa. Folks in Britain seldom encountered slavery directly and were eager to believe a narrative that these individuals were being treated fairly. Stories were told of slaves having good accommodations on the ships where they were fed, and enjoyed dancing and music. Abolishing slavery was not even a consideration to many because it was an integral part of the economy.

Too many religious leaders in the States and in Britain justified slavery with Scripture, quoting passages such as Ephesians 6:5, "Slaves, be obedient to those who are your masters according to the flesh, with fear and trembling, in the sincerity of your heart, as to Christ." In Virginia, Baptists provided education for some of the slaves and helped them start churches with their own pastors. Benevolent slave owners defended their position citing their hospitality for slaves, providing adequate housing, clothing, and food for them.

However, regardless of the narrative, slavery was horrible. There were few acts of mercy toward slaves and even the best of slave owners hardly considered slaves as their equals, created in the image and likeness of God. Slaves were tools, owned, bought and sold by individuals using them for the benefit of slave owners. The horrible circumstances of capturing slaves, separating them from their family, crowding them into boats where they were being offered only the basic elements of life; and afterwards those who survived were humiliated by being sold as objects without souls to the highest bidders, so they could be sentenced to a life of meaningless servitude exploited by heartless masters.

> "As a goldfish swimming in a bowl doesn't know what water is, so a person living in eighteenth-century Great Britain—immersed in an economic and social structure built on the slave trade—could not easily, if at all, see slavery for what it was. To do so required, it seemed, a certain kind of perceptiveness of mind and spirit, Hannah More was one of the few who possessed it."[2]

Few even imagined a world without slavery that had been around throughout human history.

> "Not only were British commerce and prosperity seen as dependent on the slave trade, but so, too, was the kingdom's military prowess. As an island nation, England relied on the health of the navy for its defense. Britain owned more than half of the world's slave ships. The slave trade provided valuable training ground for naval forces. Abolition of the slave trade would 'annihilate' an industry that put sailors and ships to work in addition to generating wealth from imports and exports, a 1791 declaration to the House of Commons asserted."[3]

Someone needed to expose the reality of the suffering of slaves to a world reluctant to hear the truth. A few courageous pastors stood up and spoke freedom for slaves such as John Newton in England, who once was a captain of a slave ship himself, and John Leland a Virginia pastor.

Christians were some of the first to express opposition to slavery in England. In 1671, the Quaker George Fox preached against it. The Puritan Richard Baxter joined in the denunciation of slavery in 1680. As we have mentioned in previously one of the leading voices a century later was Granville Sharp.

Hannah More may have done more than any other to begin to change the narrative of slaves so that people could see them as humans created in the image of God. One of her poems, "The Sorrows of Yamba; or the Negro Woman's Lamentation" (1797), was the story of an African mother seized from her family and home along with one baby at her breast and two others that were sleeping nearby. In Karen Swallow Prior's excellent biography of More, *Fierce Convictions*, she shares some of the expressions of the poem, later circulated and set to the tune of a popular ballad:

Then for love of filthy Gold,
Strait they bore me to the sea;
Cramm'd me down a Slave Ship's hold,
Where were Hundreds stow'd like me.
Naked on the Platform lying,
Now we cross the tumbling wave;
Shrieking, sickening, fainting, dying,
Deed of shame for Britons brave.

The African mother-turned-slave went on to describe the suffering and degradation they experienced on the ship until finally:

I in groaning passed the night,
And did roll my aching head;
At the break of morning light,
My poor Child was cold and dead.

The mournful mother found solace in the fact that her child's suffering had ended. She was sold to a cruel master who worked her nearly to death. She managed to escape to the sea where she contemplated suicide, but there encountered an 'English missionary Good,' who shared the gospel with her. Yamba put her trust in the Lord and was baptized. She was near death, however, and her heart was still filled with love for Africa. As the poem moved toward its conclusion, Yamba exclaimed:

Cease, ye British Sons of murder!
Cease from forging Afric's Chain;
Mock your Saviour's name no further,
Cease your savage lust of gain...
Where ye gave to war it's birth,
Where your traders fix'd their den,
There go publish 'Peace on Earth,'
Go proclaim 'good-will to men.'
Where ye once have carried slaughter,
Vice, and Slavery, and Sin;
Seiz'd on Husband, Wife, and Daughter,
Let the Gospel enter in.[4]

"By 1730, Great Britain led all other countries in the slave trade. From 1690 to the end of Britain's slave trade in 1807, at least 2.8 million African slaves were carried aboard British ships, 500,000 of them on Bristol's vessels."[5] By 1737, Bristol, More's home, became Britain's busiest slave port. "By the Victorian era, the wealth of one in six of the city's richest citizens had some connection to the slave trade...The city hosted some of the age's most renowned speakers, actors, and actresses, as well as members of the nobility."[6] It was within this context of human evil and society's finest, that God called out the third of five daughters, born to bright but humble parents, the voice of one who would help shape the culture of England.

God's providence was clearly seen in Hannah More's life as He gifted her with a brilliant mind, gave her the gift of writing, and prepared her to influence the influencers while bringing prominent individuals into her life that helped to form her and promote her work. Sir James Stonhouse, an Oxford educated clergyman and physician who began as a deist but later became an evangelical, guided More's study and readings in theology. Stonhouse sent her manuscript of the *Inflexible Captive* to the famous London actor David Garrick, who later became a close personal friend to Hannah and opened doors for her among London's elite, including Dr. Samuel Johnson.

> "For the literati, Dr. Johnson defined the age—quite literally. He was, after all, the author of the standard-setting English language dictionary, published in 1755. In addition to this pioneering work, Johnson wrote poetry, fiction, essays, biographies, and criticisms. Even now, literary scholars refer to the latter half of the eighteenth century as the age of Johnson."[7]

> "The two made an instant and vibrant connection. Although Johnson was well into his sixties, with numerous ailments, he and More developed an immediate and strong affection for each other. Johnson was impressed by More's passion and 'genuine and unaffected' personality, rare among the urbane and jaded London elite. And who didn't love the eminent Dr. Johnson?"[8]

Even though More developed a friendship with some of London's most influential leaders, she had a difficult time finding herself among such celebrated individuals.

> "Although she was no shrinking wallflower, More did not suffer from overconfidence, particularly among the elite. In some early gathering where she was introduced to some of the leading names in London, More confessed, 'I felt myself like a worm, the more a worm for the consequence which was given me by mixing with such a society.' Even after the successful production in London of her play *Percy*, she told her friend Frances Boscawen, 'I always think people will like me the less the more they see me.'"[9]

God didn't open doors for Hannah and give her natural gifts for her own edification. God had a kingdom assignment for her, desiring to use her to open the eyes of a nation to the horrors of slavery. Far too often God provides opportunities for His prophets to speak truth to power only to have them fail the occasion by speaking favorably to the king (Congressman, CEO, President, Governor, Celebrity), as did the prophets who failed to speak truth to King Jehoshaphat in 1 Kings 22:13. Only one prophet, Micaiah, was bold enough to speak the truth to the king, and the king rewarded him by throwing him in prison. If the king had listened to Micaiah, the king's life might have been spared.

> "In 1780, during the height of her high-society years in London, More read a book that changed her life. *Cardiphonia*, sometimes translated by publishers as *The Utterance of the Heart*, was a collection of letters penned by John Newton, author of 'Amazing Grace.' As was common, Newton's book was published pseudonymously."[10]

The book was full of life, unlike the dead religion found in members of the Church of England. More was anxious to meet the author. "The volume of personal letters by Newton put forth his convictions concerning human depravity and the sufficiency of Christ to redeem fallen humanity."[11]

> "More's meeting with Newton marked one more significant stone on her path toward an increasingly evangelical—and personal—faith. It was Newton—his writings, his sermons, and his friendship—who convinced More to devote her life to promoting spiritual education and reformation across British society. With Newton, in the words of his well-known hymn, More could say, I once 'was blind, but now I see.'"[12]

Former Congressman Frank Wolf told me in the early days of 21Wilberforce, "Congress cannot change culture, it is downstream for the culture. But the church can." Slavery was abolished in England by an act of the Parliament. However, that would have never happened without the decades, even centuries, of preachers, poets, and musicians calling out slavery for the evil that it was and demanding an end to the cruel practice.

In 1788, More produced the poem, "Slavery," just as Wilberforce was prepared to present a resolution to the Parliament to limit the number of slaves that could be placed in a ship. Her poem was published about the time of a pamphlet written by Newton, *Thoughts upon the African Slave Trade*, was released. "Around the same time, Newton's collaborator on his famous Olney Hymns, William Cowper, wrote his poem 'The Negro's Complaint.' Cowper was one of the most read poets of the day. Introspective and prone to bouts of depression, he wrote poetry that anticipated the coming romantic age: intense in emotion, vivid in imagery, and humane in temper."[13]

Artists were also used by God to change the narrative of slavery.

> "Nonconformist Christian Josiah Wedgwood manufactured the famous jasper medallion topped with a relief of a kneeling slave in chains and emblazoned above him the phrase 'Am I not a man and a brother?' The image was imprinted across the empire and could be found on plates, tea caddies, hairpins, bracelets, and snuffboxes. Wedgwood even sent one to Benjamin Franklin in America."[14]

The print is still used today as a tribute to the ending of slavery in England.

Overcoming injustice is not an overnight accomplishment by a single individual. God raises up emergent leaders from numerous backgrounds, disciplines, and vocations to become part of a movement that calls a nation or a community or a congregation to repentance and action. False narratives need to be exposed and truth must be addressed, laws and practices that embolden injustice overturned, and systems that promote compassion and justice installed.

The legislation abolishing slavery didn't happen until there was an outcry from the people. The years of labor from Sharp, Clarkson, Newton, More, Cowper, and Wilberforce, joined by thousands of others who remain unnamed here, finally bore the fruit of freedom, not just for those enslaved at the time, but also for the millions since then who avoided slavery altogether.

More felt hurried when she wrote the poem "Slavery." However the poem demanded empathy from those who read and heard it. "The poem's influence lasted into the next century, when it was credited with inspiring missionaries, including the famous David Livingstone, to take Christianity to Africa."[15]

The author of *Fierce Convictions*, Karen Swallow Prior, selects a few verses from "Slavery" to allow us to hear the cry of the slave and the call for God's grace.

Whene'er to Afric's shores I turn my eyes,
Horrors of deepest, deadliest guilt arise;
I see, by more than Fancy's mirror shown,
The burning village, and the blazing town:
See the dire victim torn from social life,
The shrieking babe, the agonizing wife!
She, wretch forlorn! Is dragged by hostile hands,
Transmitted miseries, and successive chains,

The sole sad heritage her child obtains.
E'en this last wretched boon their foes deny,
To weep together, or together die.
By felon hands, by one relentless stroke,
See the fond links of Nature broke!
The fibres twisting round a parent's heart,
Torn from their grasp, and bleeding as they part.

Hold murderers! Hold! Nor aggravate distress;
Respect the passions you yourself possess:
Ev'n you, of ruffian heart, and ruthless hand,
Love your own offspring, love your native land;
Ev'n you, with fond impatient feelings burn,
Though free as air, though certain of return...
Think on the wretch whose aggravated pains
To exile misery adds, to misery chains.

And Thou! Great source of Nature and of Grace,
Who of one blood didst form the human race,
Look down in mercy in thy chosen time,
With equal eye on Afric's suffering clime:
Disperse her shades of intellectual night,
Repeat they high behest—Let there be light!
Bring each benighted soul, great God, to Thee,
And with thy wide salvation make them free![16]

Endnotes

[1] The quotation appears in different forms because Niemoller often spoke extemporaneously. This is the poem as it appears at the U.S. Holocaust Museum.

[2] Karen Swallow Prior, Fierce Convictions (Manzanita, OR: Thomas Nelson, 2014), 108.

[3] Ibid., 108.

[4] Karen Swallow Prior, *Fierce Convictions*, comments and poem included in pages 131-133.

[5] Ibid., 28.

[6] Ibid., 29.

[7] Ibid., 57.

[8] Ibid., 58.

[9] Ibid., 63.

[10] Ibid., 105.

[11] Ibid., 106.

[12] Ibid., 108.

[13] Ibid., 127.

[14] Ibid., 128.

[15] Ibid., 131.

[16] Ibid., 129-130.

Conclusion

Slavery as an institution is abolished, thanks to William Wilberforce, Hannah More, President Abraham Lincoln, and a host of others. Jim Crow laws are off the books, because of the courageous leadership of Martin Luther King, Jr., Congressman John Lewis, and a cast of thousands of civil rights leaders. Yet thousands are still enslaved through human trafficking and Boko Haram in Northern Nigeria is still holding two thousand girls captive.

Emergent leaders are needed in every generation and in every community to continue to lead the fight for justice. The pandemic of 2020 combined with global social unrest, civil wars, mass migration, religious persecution, hunger, homelessness, racism, and divisive elections have created a world in crisis. Who are the leaders in this generation that are leading the struggle for justice?

The passion, expertise, and strategies of the leaders we have discussed in *Speak Freedom* are needed today as much as ever before. Some have risen to the occasion on a global stage while others work quietly on local issues. Emergent leaders are servant leaders, like the heroic nurses who put their lives on the line every day while they maintain physical contact with critically ill patients with infectious diseases. While some complain about the fatigue of having to wear masks in public places, these nurses are working overtime in stressful situations where the least error may lead to serious consequences for themselves and for the patients.

During 2020, we have met dedicated school teachers who seek innovative approaches to teaching students, NGO's providing nutritious meals to families isolated during the virus, pastors seeking to maintain contact with parishioners while providing meaningful worship experiences, political leaders seeking to preserve a balance between protecting the public and maintaining meaningful jobs, public servants providing necessary services, companies delivering products, and farmers and ranchers distributing food accessible to families. High profile situations where Blacks were killed by those hired to protect us awakened the public to inequities in law enforcement within predominantly communities of color. At the same time, heroic police feared for their own lives even though they attempted to serve with integrity.

The leaders we studied like the Apostle Paul, Wilberforce, More, King, as well as Bob Fu, Hormoz Shariat, Tillie Burgin, Ben Kwashi, and others, had many things in common. All were servant leaders guided by their faith in God who had a kingdom assignment for them. Their goal was not fame, wealth, or power; they were driven by a passion for justice that God placed on their hearts.

These emergent leaders were also competent, exercising best practices while demonstrating courage and a resilient spirit of encouraging teams to join with them in their pursuit of justice. These leaders were strategic, seeking to build collaborations with like-minded others and fighting for just laws and systems that perpetuate positive change.

What is the burden that God has burned into your heart? Are you willing to pay the price for a lifetime of honing the skills required for making a difference? Are you ready to face the criticism that Wilberforce encountered or even martyrdom like King? Are you willing to set aside personal ambition and recognition for the privilege of serving those without a voice? I pray God will continue to bless those of you who are already leading the battle for justice. I also pray that others may find inspiration for the journey from the men and women highlighted in this book who found fulfillment in living life in the center of God's will.

Jesus made His mission very clear at the beginning of His ministry when He spoke to his neighbors in Nazareth: "The Spirit of the Lord is upon Me, because He anointed Me to preach the gospel to the poor. He has sent Me to proclaim release to the captives, and recovery of sight to the blind, to set free those who are oppressed, to proclaim the favorable year of the Lord" (Luke 4:18-19).

May God bless you as you dare *Speak Freedom* to a world desperate for the hope and love of Christ.

Acknowledgments

When I had the privilege of serving as Executive Director of Texas Baptists I visited with numerous church committees who were searching for their next pastor. Obviously they desired someone who had a vibrant relationship with the Lord and one who shared their theological principles. Inspirational preaching and other pastoral competencies were expected. However, these committees almost all stated early in the conversations they wanted someone who would lead them.

Effective leadership is a central component to transformational impact. When the team of researches led by Jim Collins was examining the few companies that moved their enterprises from being good organizations to becoming great, Collins was not looking for the key to be leadership, yet the empirical evidence was clear---the great companies were led by individuals who shared similar traits Collins identified as Level 5 Leaders.

I have the privilege of learning from the writings and relationships with very effective leaders. Dr. Harvey Perkins, CEO of the Urban Learning And Leadership Center in Newport News, Virginia, was one of those. When I became his pastor we compared notes, ideas and books that we were reading about leadership. Harvey is an educator, having served as a teacher, a principal and assistant superintendent of schools. He witnessed the challenges facing public education and began providing training for teachers and administrators of school districts in transition because of shifts in demographics or changing expectations.

Dr. Perkins introduced me to the work of Kouzes and Posner, *The Leadership Challenge*, and we began to use some of their vast resources for training conferences among churches, seminary students, and even public regional conferences. Each of us brought his own experiences and stories to the training as we encouraged others to join us as we sought to implement best practices while fulfilling our vocational assignments.

As I reflect on the many who have shaped my understanding of leadership, I realize the primary influence for me was my father, Kenneth Everett. I observed his life as a follower of Christ, husband, dad, grandfather, pastor and community leader; I knew I wanted to be like him. Even as I became an adult, he was the one I often called first when I needed wisdom for a challenging situation.

My wife Sheila continues to be my primary partner in life and ministry. We have shared life together as pastor and wife, co-founders of a seminary, leaders in denominational work and she is my inspiration, encourager and chief counselor in our work with 21Wilberforce. I continue to learn from our two adult children, Jeremy and Rachel, who are also very effective leaders and champions for justice.

I am grateful for our staff at 21Wilberforce for our partnership together with those facing religious oppression and am thankful for their encouragement and input during my writing of *Speak Freedom*.

Bob Billups, the publisher of BaptistWay Press, has been an active participant with me throughout the writing and the editing of this book. He has gone beyond what is expected of a publisher to assist in preparing a book that we pray will be a helpful tool for those continuing to emerge in their roles as leaders.

I want to give a special shout out to Susie Jaynes who has not only served as an editor of the book, but has also been a thought partner with me as we sought to offer encouragement and resources for emerging leaders.

God has allowed Sheila and me to serve some amazing churches and institutions. Along the way we have become friends with folks who love God and hate injustice. We continue to seek to follow Christ and the teachings of His Word as we aspire to "do justice, love mercy and walk humbly with our God" (Micah 6:8).

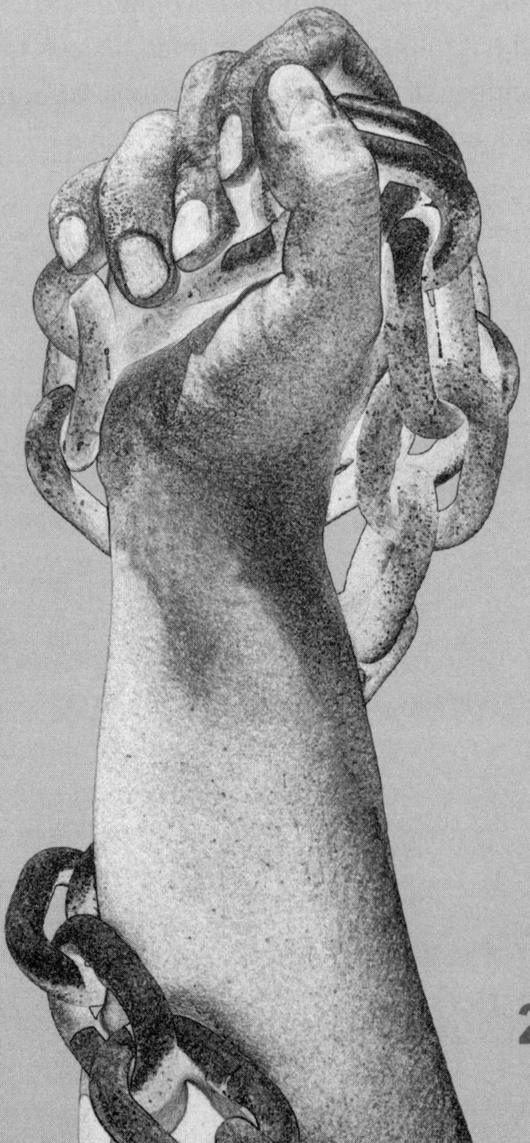